1 MONTH OF
FREE
READING

at
www.ForgottenBooks.com

By purchasing this book you are eligible for one month membership to ForgottenBooks.com, giving you unlimited access to our entire collection of over 1,000,000 titles via our web site and mobile apps.

To claim your free month visit:
www.forgottenbooks.com/free64868

ISBN 978-1-5285-6607-0
PIBN 10064868

PREFATORY NOTE.

THIS manual is intended for use in schools, and in colleges which have not yet been able to make room in their curricula for a more complete course of political study. It is one chapter — the longest — extracted from a volume which I have just published entitled *The State: Elements of Historical and Practical Politics*, — a work devoted to a somewhat extended sketch of the history of political institutions, to detailed descriptions of representative modern governments, and to brief discussions of the main lessons as to the nature of the state and of law to be drawn from a study of comparative politics. Sectional references in the body of the present text which are marked with an *asterisk* refer to sections of the larger work. Except for changes in the numbering of its own paragraphs, this text stands exactly as it is in the volume of which it forms a part.

I believe that it will be found that this book, though not originally prepared for separate publication, is fitted to play an independent rôle in class use without embarrassment. The prominence given by it to the state governments ought to recommend it, I should think, to those who are discovering, with the ablest of our critics, that the states are the vital and essential units of our great national system.

WOODROW WILSON.

MIDDLETOWN, CONN.,
    Aug. 22, 1889.

TOPICAL ANALYSIS.

———◆◇◆———

TOPICAL ANALYSIS.

THE GOVERNMENT OF THE UNITED STATES.

1. **The English Occupation of America.** — The political institutions of the United States are in all their main features simply the political institutions of England, as transplanted by English colonists in the course of the two centuries which preceded our own, worked out through a fresh development to new and characteristic forms. Though now possessing so large an admixture of foreign blood, a large majority of the people of the United States are still of British extraction ; and at first the settlements of New England and the South contained no other element. In the far North, in what is now Canada, there were French settlements; in Florida there were colonists from Spain, and at the mouth of the Mississippi also there was a French population; the Dutch had settled upon the Hudson and held the great port at its mouth, and the Swedes had established themselves on the Delaware : all along the coast there was rivalry between the western nations of Europe for the possession of the new continent. But by steady and for the most part easy steps of aggression the English extended their domain and won the best regions of the great coast. New England, Virginia, and the Carolinas were never seriously disputed against them; and, these once possessed, the intervening foreigner was soon thrust out : so that the English power had presently a compact and centred mass which could not be dislodged, and whose ultimate expansion over the whole continent it proved impossible to stay. England was not long in

widening her colonial borders: the French power was crushed out in the North, the Spanish power was limited in the South, and the colonies had only to become free to develop energy more than sufficient to make all the most competed-for portions of the continent thoroughly English, — thoroughly Anglo-American.

2. **Adaptation of English Institutions.** — This growth of the English power in America involved as of course a corresponding expansion of English local institutions of government; as America became English, English institutions in the colonies became American: they adapted themselves, *i.e.*, to the new problems and the new conveniences of political life in separate colonies, — colonies struggling at first, then expanding, at last triumphing; and without losing their English character gained an American form and flavor.

3. It would be an utterly erroneous, an entirely reversed, statement of our colonial history to say that the English planted states in America: they planted small isolated settlements, and these settlements grew into states. The process, in other words, was from local, through state, to national organization. And not everywhere among the English on the new continent was the form of local government at first adopted the same: there was no invariable pattern, but everywhere, on the contrary, a spontaneous adjustment of political means to place and circumstance. By all the settlements alike English precedent was followed, but not the same English precedent; each colony, with the true English sagacity of practical habit, borrowed what was best suited to its own situation. New England had one system, Virginia another, New Jersey and Pennsylvania still a third, compounded after a sort of the other two.

4. **The New England Colonies.** — In New England the centre of government was always the town, with its church and schoolhouse and its neighborly cluster of houses gathered about these. The soil on the coast where the first settlers established

themselves was shallow and slow to yield returns even to hard and assiduous toil; the climate was rigorous, with its long winters and its bleak coast winds; every circumstance invited to close settlement and trade, to the intimate relationships of commerce and the adventures of sea-faring rather than to the wide-spreading settlements characteristic of an agricultural population.

5.   The first New Englanders, moreover, were religious refugees.   They had left the Old World to escape the Old World's persecutions and in order to find independence of worship; they were establishing a church as well as a community; they acted as organized congregations; their life was both spiritually and temporally organic.   Close geographical association, therefore, such as was virtually forced upon them by the conditions of livelihood by which they found themselves constrained, accorded well with their higher social purposes. The church could be made, by such association, and accordingly was made, the vital nerve-centre of their union: the minister was the ruling head of the community, and church membership was in several of the settlements recognized as identical with citizenship.

6.   **The Separate Towns.** — The several parts of the New England coast were settled by quite independent groups of settlers.   There was the Plymouth colony at Plymouth, and altogether distinct from it, the Massachusetts Bay colony at Salem and Charlestown.   To the south of these, founded by men dissatisfied with the Massachusetts government, were Portsmouth, Newport, and Providence, in what is now Rhode Island.   On the Connecticut river other wanderers from Massachusetts built Hartford and Windsor and Wethersfield.   Saybrook, at the mouth of the Connecticut river, was settled direct from England; so also was the colony of New Haven, on the coast of Long Island Sound west of the Connecticut.   From year to year the planting of towns went diligently on: almost every town became the prolific mother of towns, which either sprang

up close about it and retained a sort of dependence upon it, or, planted at a distance, ventured upon an entirely separate life in the wilderness.

7. **Union of the Towns.** — Gradually the towns of each of the general regions mentioned drew together into the colonies known to later times, the colonies which were to form the Union. Plymouth merged in Massachusetts; Portsmouth, Newport, and Providence became but parts of Rhode Island; New Haven was joined to Connecticut. But at first these larger colonies were scarcely more than town leagues: each town retained unaltered its separate organization and a perfect independence in the regulation of its own local affairs. In Rhode Island, particularly, their jealousy of each other and their reluctance to expose themselves to anything like a loss of perfect autonomy long kept the common government which they most of the time maintained at a balance between union and dissolution. In the other New England colonies the same influences manifested themselves, though in a less degree. The town system which everywhere prevailed was by its nature an extremely decentralized form of government: government, so to say, came to a separate head in each locality: and the chief vitality was in these several self-governing units of each group rather than in the bonds which connected them with each other.

8. **Forms of Town Government.** — The form of town government was everywhere such as it was quite natural that Englishmen should have set up. The names of the town officers were borrowed from the borough governments at home, and their duties were, as nearly as circumstances warranted, the same as the duties of the officers whose names they bore. But the New England town was, at the same time, in many of its most important and most characteristic features, rather a reversion to older types of government than a transplanted cutting of the towns which the settlers had left behind them in the England of the seventeenth century. There was in it

of course none of the elaborated class privilege that narrowed the town governments of the England of that time. All the townsmen met in town meeting and there elected their officers: those officers were responsible to them and always rendered careful account of their actions to the body which elected them. Generally the most important of these officers were called Selectmen, — men selected by the town meeting to carry on the necessary public business of the community, — and these Selectmen stood in the closest relations of counsel and responsibility to the town meeting. In the earliest times the franchise was restricted, in Massachusetts and New Haven at least, to those who were church members, and many were excluded by this rule from participation in the government; but even under such circumstances there was real and effective self-government. The towns lacked neither vitality nor energy, for they did not lack liberty. In the late days when great cities grew up, the simple township system had to be abandoned in part; as the colonies expanded, too, they gained in energy and vitality as wholes, and their component parts, the towns, fell by degrees to a place of less exclusive importance in colonial affairs; but this basis of the township was never lost and is to-day still the foundation of local government in New England.

9. **Colonial Organization.** — As the towns came together into the groupings which constituted the later colonies other areas of government of course came into use. Townships were, for judicial purposes, combined into counties, and by various other means of organization a new nexus was given to the several parts of the now extended state. From the first the colonists had their "general courts," their central legislative assemblies representative of the freemen. To these assemblies went delegates from the several towns comprised in the colony. As the colonies grew, their growth but strengthened their assemblies: it was in the common ruling function of these that the union of the several parts of each colony was made real and lasting.

The sheriffs of the counties of colonial Massachusetts were appointed by the Governor. The development of the county organization brought into existence, too, Justices of the Peace who met in Quarter Sessions, afterwards called "General Sessions," and who were the general county authority quite after the fashion of the mother country.[1]

10. **The Southern Colonies.** — To this picture of the political institutions of colonial New England political and social organization in the Southern colonies offered many broad contrasts. The settlers in Virginia were not religious refugees : they had come out for a separate adventure in political, or rather in social, organization, but not for a separate venture in religion; and the coast they happened upon, instead of being rugged and bleak, was low and fertile, with a kindly climate, deep rivers, broad stretches of inviting country, and a generous readiness to yield its fruits in season. They had been sent out by a Company (the "Virginia Company" it was called) in England, to which the Virginia territory had been granted by the Crown, and they had no thought but to live under the governors whom the Company had placed over them. They founded Jamestown some hundred miles above the mouth of the James river; but Jamestown was in no way like the New England towns, and it soon became evident that town life was not to be the characteristic life of the colony. The rich soil invited to agriculture, the numerous rivers, full and deep, stood ready to serve as natural highways, and as the population of the colony increased it spread, — spread far and wide along the courses of the rivers.

11. **Expansion without Separation.** — Still there would appear to have been no idea of organic separation in this process, as there was so often in the spreadings of the New England colonists. Great plantations indeed grew up with an almost entirely separate life of their own, with their own wharves on

[1] See *Town and County Government in the English Colonies of North America*, by Edward Channing, Johns Hopkins University Studies in Historical and Political Science, 2d Series, pp. 40–42.

the river fronts and their own direct trade with the outer world by vessels which came and went between them and England, or between them and the trading colonies to the north; but all this took place without any idea of organic political separateness.   This diffused agricultural population thus living its own life on the great rural properties which steadily multiplied in all directions still consciously formed a single colony, living at first under the general government of the Company which had sent out the first settlers, and afterwards, when the Company had been deprived of its charter and possessions, under the authority of royal governors.   Its parts hung loosely together indeed, but they did not threaten to fall apart : the plan was expansion, not segregation.

12.   **Southern Colonial Society.** — The characteristics of the society formed under such circumstances were of course very marked.   Slaves were early introduced into the colony, and served well to aid and quicken the development of the plantation system.   A great gap speedily showed itself between the owners of estates and the laboring classes.   Where slavery exists manual toil must be considered slavish and all the ideas on which aristocracy are founded must find easy and spontaneous rootage.   Great contrasts of condition soon appeared, such as the more democratic trading communities of New England were not to know until the rise of the modern industrial organization; and the governing power rested of course with the powerful, the propertied classes.

13.   **Government of Colonial Virginia.** — The government of colonial Virginia bore, in all its broader features, much the same character as the rural government of England.   Organization was effected through a machinery of wide counties, instead of by means of compacted townships.   There was at the head of each county, under this first order of things, a Lieutenant whose duties corresponded roughly with those of the Lords Lieutenant in England.   The other important executive officer of the county, too, in Virginia as in England,

was the Sheriff. The Lieutenant was appointed by the Governor, was chief of the military (militia) organization of the county, and, by virtue of his membership in the Governor's Council, exercised certain judicial functions in the county. The Sheriff also was appointed by the Governor, upon the nomination of the Justices of the county. His duties an English sheriff would have regarded as quite normal. And added to these officers there was, as in England, a "commission of the peace," a body of justices or commissioners authorized to hold county court for the hearing of all ordinary cases not of grave import; authorized to levy the county taxes, to appoint surveyors of highways, to divide the county into precincts; empowered to act as the general administrative authority of the county in the management of all matters not otherwise assigned. The Episcopal church had the same official recognition in Virginia as in England and contributed the same machinery, — the machinery of the Vestry, — to local government. Even the division of the 'hundred' was recognized, so close was the outline likeness between the institutions of the mother country and those of her crude child in the west. The system was undemocratic, of course, as was its model: "the dominant idea," as Mr. Ingle says, "was gradation of power from the Governor *downward*, not upward from the people."[1] The Justices, like the other officers of the county, were appointed by the Governor, and held only during his pleasure : the whole system rested upon a rather absolute centralization. But still there was liberty. There was strong local feeling and individual pride to counteract the subserviency of the officers : those officers showed a more or less self-respecting independence in their administration; and at least the spirit of English self-government was kept alive.

---

[1] *Local Institutions in Virginia*, by Edward Ingle, Johns Hopkins University Studies in Historical and Political Science, 3d Series, p. 97 (continuous, p. 199).

14. **Virginia's Colonial Assembly.** — The vital centre of the political life of the colony was her representative assembly. So early as 1619, but twelve years after the foundation of the colony (1607), the Virginia Company, then still in control, had called together in the colony, through its governor, an assembly representing the plantations then existing, which were in this way treated as independent corporations entitled to a representative voice in colonial affairs. Later years saw the Assembly developed upon the basis of a representation by towns, hundreds, and plantations: and even after the governors sent out by the Company had been supplanted by royal governors this representative body, this House of Burgesses, as it came to be styled, continued to exist, and to wax strong in control. The first Assembly, that of 1619, had sat in joint session with the governor and his council, but the more fully developed assembly of later times sat apart as a distinct and independent body. It was this elective representation in the government of the colony which made and kept Virginia a vital political unit, with a real organic life and feeling.

15. **The constitutions of the other southern colonies** corresponded in all essential features with the constitution of Virginia. They, too, had the county system and the general representation in a central assembly, combined with governors and councils appointed by the Crown. All save Maryland. Her constitution differed from the others mainly in this, that in place of the king stood a 'proprietor' to whom the fullest prerogatives of government had been granted.

16. **The Middle Colonies** had a mixed population. New York had been New Amsterdam, and the Delaware had been first settled by the Swedes and then conquered by the Dutch. When the territory, which was to comprise New York, New Jersey, Delaware, and Pennsylvania, fell into the hands of the English the foreign element was not displaced but merely dominated; and to a large extent it kept its local peculiarities of institution. For the rest, the English settlers of the region

followed no uniform or characteristic method of organization. The middle colonies, though possessed of a rich soil, had also fine seaports which invited to commerce; their climate was neither so harsh as that of New England, nor so mild and beguiling as that of the southern colonies. Their people, consequently, built towns and traded, like the people of New England; but also spread abroad over the fertile country and farmed, like the people of Virginia. They did these things, however, without developing either the town system of New England or the plantation system of Virginia. Townships they had, but counties also; they were simple and democratic, like the New Englanders, and yet they were agricultural also, like the Virginians: in occupation and political organization, as well as in geographical situation, they were midway between their neighbors to the north and south.

17. **The Charters: Massachusetts.** — The political relations of the colonies to the mother country during the various developments of which I have spoken were as various as the separate histories of the colonies. The three New England colonies, Massachusetts, Rhode Island, and Connecticut, possessed charters from the king which virtually authorized them to conduct their own governments without direct interference on the part of the Administration at home. During the first years of English settlement on the American coast it had been the practice of the government in England to grant territory on the new continent to companies like the Virginia Company of which I have spoken, — grants which carried with them the right of governing the new settlements subject only to a general supervision on the part of the home authorities. The colony of Massachusetts Bay was established under such an arrangement: a Company, to which special privileges of settlement and government had been granted, sent out colonists who founded Salem and Charlestown; but the history of this Company was very different from the history of the Virginia Company. The Virginia Company tried to manage their colony

from London, where the members of the Company, who were active liberals and therefore not very active courtiers, presently got into trouble with the government and had both their charter and their colony taken away from them.   The Massachusetts Company, on the other hand, itself came to America, and, almost unobserved by the powers in London, erected something very like a separate state on the new continent.   Its charter was received in 1629; in 1630 it emigrated, governor, directors, charter, and all, to America, bringing a numerous body of settlers, founded Boston and Cambridge, and put quietly into operation the complete machinery of government which it had brought with it.   It created not a little stir in official circles in England when it was discovered that the Company which had been given rights of settlement on the New England coast had left the country and was building a flourishing semi-independent state on its territories; but small colonies at a great distance could not long retain the attention of busy politicians in London, and nothing was done then to destroy the bold arrangement.   Fatal collision with the home government could not, however, it turned out, be permanently, or even long avoided by the aggressive, self-willed rulers of the Massachusetts Company.   Many of the laws which they passed did not please the Crown, — particularly those which set up an exclusive religion and tolerated no other; they would not change their laws at the Crown's bidding; and, though the evil day was postponed, it came at last.   In 1684 the contest between Crown and colony came to a head, and the charter of the Massachusetts Company was annulled.   Before a change could be effected in the government, indeed, the king, Charles II., died, and during the troublous reign of James II. the colonists quietly resumed their charter privileges; but in 1692 the government of William and Mary was ready to deal with them, and a new form of colonial organization was forced upon them. They were compelled to take a governor from the king; the royal governor appointed the judicial officers of the colony and

controlled its military forces ; and, although the colonists retained their assembly and through that assembly chose the
governor's Council,. the old charter privileges were permanently lost.

18. **The Connecticut Charter.** — Rhode Island and Connecticut were small and more fortunate. The town of Saybrook, at the mouth of the Connecticut river, had been founded
under a charter granted to two English noblemen, and consisted,
therefore, of immigrants direct from England ; but Saybrook
did not grow rapidly and proved a comparative failure. The
successful and dominant settlement on the Connecticut was
that which had been founded higher up the river at Hartford
by men from Massachusetts who had neither charter nor any
other legal rights, but who had simply come, settled, and made
a written constitution for themselves. New Haven, westward
of the river on the shore of the sound, had been established
by a band of English immigrants equally without charter
rights, but equally ready and able to construct a frame of government for themselves. Some thirty years after their settlement, the leaders of the 'Connecticut colony,' up the river,
which meantime had become an extended cluster of towns,
decided that it was time to obtain a charter. Accordingly
they sent their governor, Winthrop, to England to procure
one. He was entirely successful, much more successful than
was pleasant to the settlers of the New Haven district ; for he
had obtained a grant which included their lands and colony
and which thus forced them to become a part of 'Connecticut.'
Saybrook had already been absorbed. The charter gave the
colonists substantially the same rights of self-government that
they had had under their own written constitution, adopted
upon their first settlement ; it was, in other words, just such
a charter as Massachusetts then enjoyed. And, unlike Massachusetts, Connecticut kept her charter, kept it not only through
colonial times to the Revolution, but made it at the Revolution
her state constitution, and was content to live under it until

1818. Her shrewdness, her arts of timely concession, and her inoffensive size enabled her to turn away from herself each successive danger of forfeiture.

19. **Rhode Island's Charter.** — Rhode Island was similarly protected by fortune and sagacious management. Roger Williams, the energetic leader of settlement in that region, obtained a charter from Parliament in 1644, which was confirmed in 1654, and replaced by a new charter, from Charles II., in 1663, the year after Connecticut obtained its legal privileges through the instrumentality of Winthrop. As New Haven and Connecticut were joined by Winthrop's charter, so were the towns of the Rhode Island country united by the charters obtained by Williams, under the style 'Rhode Island and Providence Plantations,' — a title which is still the full official name of the state. The charter of '63 was retained by the people of Rhode Island even longer than the people of Connecticut retained theirs. It was not radically changed until 1842.

20. **Proprietary Governments.** — The governments of almost all the other colonies were at first 'proprietary'; those of Maryland, Pennsylvania, and Delaware remained proprietary until the Revolution. Maryland was granted to the Calverts, Lords Baltimore; Pennsylvania and Delaware were both included in the grant to William Penn; New York was bestowed upon James, Duke of York, upon whose ascension of the throne, as James II., it became an immediate province of the Crown; New Jersey, originally a part of New York, was first bestowed by the Duke of York on Lord John Berkeley and Sir John Cartaret, was afterwards divided, then sold in part, and finally surrendered to the Crown (1702); the Carolinas and Georgia in the same way, given at first to proprietors, passed very soon into the hands of the royal government. New Hampshire, after several attempts to unite with Massachusetts, fell quietly into the status of a royal colony, without having had either a charter or a proprietary stage of existence.

21.   Government under proprietors meant simply government by governors and councils appointed by the proprietors, with in all cases a full right on the part of the people to control the government through representative assemblies. The private proprietors, like the great public proprietor, the Crown, granted charters to their colonies. The charter which Penn bestowed upon Pennsylvania is distinguished as one of the best-conceived and most liberal charters of the time; and under it his colony certainly enjoyed as good government as most of the colonies could secure.

22.   **Direct Government by the Crown,** which came in turn to every colony except Rhode Island, Connecticut, Maryland, Pennsylvania, and Delaware, involved the appointment of governors by the Crown, and also, everywhere except in Massachusetts, the appointment of the governor's council. It generally involved also the dependence of the colonial judiciary, and in general of the whole administrative machinery of government, upon the royal will; but it, nevertheless, did not exclude the colonists from substantial powers of self-government. Everywhere legislators disciplined governors with the effective whip of the money power, and everywhere the people grew accustomed to esteem the management of their own affairs, especially the control of their own taxes, matter-of-course privileges, quite as inalienable rights of Englishmen in America as of Englishmen in England.

23.   **Development of the Assemblies.** — It was, indeed, as a matter of course rather than as a matter of right that the powers of the colonial assemblies waxed greater and greater from year to year. Parliament would have been wise to continue the policy of neglect which had been the opportunity of the colonies in the development of their constitutional liberties. Left to themselves, they quickly showed what race they were of.

As Burke said, in their justification, they " had formed within themselves, either by royal instruction or royal charter, assemblies so exceedingly resembling a parliament, in all their forms, functions, and powers, that it was impossible they should not imbibe some opinion of a similar authority.

"At the first designation of these assemblies, they were probably not intended for anything more (nor perhaps did they think themselves much higher) than the municipal corporations within this island, to which some at present love to compare them. But nothing in progression can rest on its original plan. . . . Therefore, as the colonies prospered and increased to a numerous and mighty people, spreading over a very great tract of the globe, it was natural that they should attribute to assemblies so respectable in their formal constitution some part of the dignity of the great nations which they represented. No longer tied to by-laws, these assemblies made acts of all sorts and in all cases whatsoever. They levied money, not for parochial purposes, but upon regular grants to the crown, following all the rules and principles of a parliament, to which they approached every day more and more nearly. . . . Things could not be otherwise; and English colonies must be had on these terms, or not had at all. In the meantime neither party felt any inconvenience from this double legislature,[1] to which they had been formed by imperceptible habits, and old custom, the great support of all the governments in the world. Though these two legislatures were sometimes found perhaps performing the very same functions, they did not very grossly or systematically clash. . . . A regular revenue, by the authority of Parliament, for the support of civil and military establishments, seems not to have been thought of until the colonies were too proud to submit, too strong to be forced, too enlightened not to see all the consequences which must arise from such a system."[2]

24. In such assertions of a right of parliamentary self-government it might be expected that the charter colonies would be most forward; but, as a matter of fact, such was not the case. Massachusetts was ever, indeed, very stubbornly and heroically attached to her liberties, but the royal colony of Virginia was not a whit behind her. The assemblies of the royal colonies, no less than those of the charter governments, early, and as if by an instinct and habit common to the race, de-

---

[1] The legislature of England, *i.e.*, and a colonial legislature.
[2] "Letter to the Sheriffs of Bristol," *Works* (ed. Boston, 1880), Vol. II., pp. 232, 233.

veloped a consciousness and practice of local sovereignty, which comported well enough, indeed, with perfect loyalty, which was long-suffering as towards Navigation Acts and all interferences by the mother country with the external relations of the colonies, their place in the politics and commerce of the outside world, but which was from the first prompt to resent and resist all dictation as to the strictly interior affairs of the settlements. And the same was true of the proprietary colonies, also: Maryland assumed the same privileges that Virginia insisted upon enjoying, and even Pennsylvania, with its population compounded of English, Dutch, and Swedes, manifested not a little of the same spirit of independent self-direction.

25. **Development of Constitutional Liberty in the Colonies.** — There was, therefore, a comparatively uniform development of constitutional liberty throughout the colonies. Everywhere the same general causes were operative. The settlement and development of a new country gave to the elective governing bodies of the colonies a wide and various duty of legislative regulation; the newness of the country created everywhere substantially the same new conditions of social relationship; everywhere, and more and more as the years went on, there was a very general participation in communal and colonial affairs by the mass of the people most interested: democratic institutions brought in their train equality of law and a widespread consciousness of community of interest. Each colony grew the while more and more vividly conscious of its separate political personality in its relations with the other colonies and with the ruling powers in England.

26. **Political Sympathy of the Colonies.** — The substantial identity of the lines of institutional development in the several colonies appears in nothing more clearly or conclusively than in their close and spontaneous alliance against England at the Revolution. Despite very considerable outward differences of social condition and many apparent divergencies

of interest as between colony and colony, they one and all *wanted the same revolution:* almost without hesitation they ran together to co-operate by the same means for the same ends; they did not so much *make* a common cause as *have* a common cause from the first.   The real concrete case of revolution, so to say, was made up between England and Massachusetts: to the politicians in the mother country it seemed possible to divide the colonies on grounds of self-interest: apparently colonies so utterly different in every outward aspect, so strongly contrasted in actual economic condition as Massachusetts and Virginia, could easily be played off against one another.   But we now know how little foundation of fact such a view had. Boston's trade was offered to Salem, her commercial rival, as a bait to catch Salem's acquiescence in the iniquitous Boston Port Bill which shut Boston off from all trade ; but Salem would not have it : what was to prevent similar treatment of herself in the future ?   More striking still, distant Virginia sounded the call to revolution in behalf of Massachusetts : the contest was *political,* she clearly perceived, not economical, — a contest of principle, not a contest for any temporary interest or momentary advantage ; from the point of view of politics Massachusetts' quarrel was Virginia's also.   Virginia spoke at once, therefore, and as a leader, for combination, for a joint resistance to the aggressions of the home government, and at length for independence and a perpetual union between the colonies.   For the shortest possible time did the struggle remain local ; immediately it became 'continental.'

27. **American as compared with English Constitutional Development.** — There was in this development of self-government in America a certain very close resemblance to the development of self-government in England ; but there were also other points of very strong and obvious contrast between the institutional histories of the two countries.   Both in England and America the process of institutional growth was in the same direction : it began with small, hardy, deep-rooted local insti-

tutions, with small self-directing communities, and widened
from these to national institutions which bound the constituent
communities together in a strong and lasting central union.
England began with her village communities and her judicial
'hundreds,' with the primitive communal institutions of the
Teutonic folk; these were first gathered to a head in the petty
kingdoms of the days of the Saxon Heptarchy; another step,
and these one-time petty kingdoms were merely the counties
of a wider union, and England was ready for the amalgamation
of the Norman rule, was ready for the growth of her parlia-
ments and her nationality. In like manner, the United States
began with isolated settlements upon a long coast, settlements
separate, self-contained, self-regulative; these in time merged
in numerous petty colonial states; and finally these colonial
states fitted themselves together into a national union.

28. **Process of Growth in America Federation, in England
Consolidation.** — But the means of integration were in the two
cases quite diverse. American integration has been federal;
English, absorptive, incorporative. The earlier stages of federation did not appear in the southern colonies; because there
the unity of the first settlement was generally not broken; the
Virginia of the Revolution was but an expansion of the Jamestown settlement; growth by agricultural development was not
disintegrating like growth by town establishment. But in
New England the process is obviously federative from the first,
finding its most perfect type, probably, in Rhode Island, whose
town atoms drew so slowly and reluctantly together and so long
stoutly resisted the idea that they had in any sense been
absorbed or subordinated under the operation of the charters
of 'Rhode Island and Providence Plantations.' What was at
first mere confederation between these smallest units, however,
by degrees became virtual coalescence, and the absorbed towns
finally formed but subordinate parts in the new and larger
colonial units which drew together in the Continental Congresses. Between these larger units, these full-grown colonial

states, of course, union was from the first distinctly federative, matter of concession and contract. They were united in entirely voluntary association, as of course the Saxon kingdoms were not.

29. Conscious Development of Institutions in America. —Throughout their development, therefore, the colonies presented, in still another equally important respect, a marked contrast to English development in this, that the formulation of their institutions was conscious and deliberate. The royal colonies, like the proprietary and the charter colonies, exercised their rights of self-government under written grants of privilege from the Crown: their institutions grew within the area of written constituent law; from the first they had definite written 'constitutions' wherein the general fabric of their governments was outlined. Constitution by written law, therefore, became very early one of the matter-of-course habits of colonial thought and action. When they cast off their allegiance to Great Britain their self-constitution, as independent political bodies, took the shape of a recasting of their colonial constitutions simply; Rhode Island and Connecticut, as we have seen, did not even find it necessary to change their charters in any important particular: they already chose their own governors and officials as well as made their own laws. The other colonies, with little more trouble, found adequate means of self-government in changes which involved hardly more than substituting the authority of the people for the authority of the English Crown. But the charter, the written constituent law, was retained as of course: the new governments had their charters which emanated from the people, as the old governments had had theirs given by the king. Popular conventions took the place of the Privy Council. The colonists were not inventing written constitutions; they were simply continuing their former habitual constitutional life.

30. English Law and Precedent. — Whatever the form of colonial institutions, however, their substance and content were thoroughly English. In a sense, indeed, even the forms of colonial constituent law may be said to have been English, since it was English practice which originated the idea and habit of giving written grants of privilege to distant colonies. The colonial law of Canada and Australia stands to-day in much the same relation to the law of the mother country that the law of the American colonies bore to the law which created them (sec. 826). Within the constitutions of the colonial and revolutionary time, at any rate, English law and precedent were closely followed. The English common law has gone with Englishmen to the ends of the world: the English communities in America were but projected parts of the greater English community at home; the laws of private and personal relation which obtained in England were recognized and administered also in the colonies; and when, at the time of the Revolution, the colonists developed out of their charters the constitutions under which they were to live as independent commonwealths their first care was to adopt this common law under which they had always acted. Important modifications were made indeed in the law thus adopted. It was purged of all class privilege, of all church prerogative, of all things incompatible with the simple democratic society of the new world; but no real break was made with the principles of English legal precedent and practice.

31. Quite as naturally and quite as completely was English practice adhered to in the public law of the colonies and of the independent commonwealths into which they grew. The relations of the colonial legislatures with the colonial governors were just the relations of King and Parliament reproduced on a small scale, but with scarcely less earnestness and spirit. In all respects, except that of the erection of a responsible ministry representing and shielding the Executive, the relations of the people to their governments remind of English precedent. The powers of the executive were, in small, the powers of the Crown. The courts were constituted as the English courts

were, and followed the same rules of procedure. Of course the English in America, being men of the same practical political race as Englishmen in England, struck out not a few lines of development of their own in suiting their institutions to the daily needs of a new civilization and to novel conditions of social organization; American politics were not long in acquiring in many respects a character peculiarly their own. But the manner of development was English throughout: there was nowhere any turning of sharp corners: there was nowhere any break of continuity: to the present day our institutions rest upon foundations as old as the Teutonic peoples.

32. **Union: Preliminary Steps.** — How much of political precedent that was their own the colonists had developed appeared most distinctly when they came to put the timbers of their Union together in the days succeeding the Revolution. The colonies cannot be said to have framed any federative constituent law until 1777, when the Articles of Confederation were drawn up. Before that time they had co-operated without any determinate law of co-operation, acting rather upon the suggestions of international procedure than upon any clear recognition of corporate combination. Preparations for union there had been, and signs of its coming; but no more. For a period of forty years following the year 1643 the New England colonies had held together in loose confederation against the Indians; in 1754 colonial delegates who had met at Albany for conference with representatives of the Six Nations discussed a premature plan of union; in 1765 delegates from nine of the colonies met at New York and uttered in behalf of all English Americans that protest against taxation by Parliament which gave the key-note to all the subsequent thought of the revolutionary movement; and in 1774 sat the first of the series of 'Continental Congresses' with which began American union. But in none of these steps was there any creation of organic union: that was to be the result of slow processes, and was to be effected only by the formulation of an entirely new body of law.

33. **Separateness of the Colonial Governments.** — It is very important, if a just view is to be formed of the processes by which the Union was constructed, to realize the complete separateness of the governments of the colonies. They all held substantially the same general relation to the English authorities; they had a common duty as towards the distant country from which they had all come out; but they were not connected by any bonds of government on this side the sea. Each of the colonies had its own separate executive officials, legislature, and courts, which had no connection whatever with the officers, legislatures, and courts of any other colony. Their co-operation from time to time in meeting dangers which threatened them all alike was natural and spontaneous, but it was intermittent; it rested upon mere temporary necessity and had no basis of interior organic law. The colonists had many grounds of sympathy. Besides possessing the same blood and the same language, they entertained the same ideas about political justice; their dangers, whether proceeding from aggressions on the part of the French and Indians which threatened their lives, or from aggressions by Parliament which threatened their liberties, were common dangers: they were one and all equally interested in the successful development and liberal government of the new country with which they had identified themselves. But the motive of their endeavors was always the preservation of their internal and separate self-government; their liberties were historically coincident with their organization and rights as separate governments. It was, therefore, only by the slow processes of a hard experience of the fatal consequences of any other course that the colonies were brought to subordinate themselves to a central authority which could go further than mere conference and command them. They saw from the first the necessity for co-operation, but they did not see from the first the absolute necessity for union. Very slowly, considering the swift influences of revolution amidst which they worked, and very reluctantly, considering the evident dangers of separation which daily looked them in the face, did they construct the union which was to deprive them of the fulness of their loved independence.

34. **The Confederation.** — It was not until 1781 that a foundation of distinct written law was put beneath the practice of union; it was not till 1789 that the law of the union was made organic. In 1781 the Articles of Confederation were finally adopted which had been proposed by the Continental Congress of 1777: but these Articles gave no real integration

to the constituent states: they were from the first a rope of sand which could bind no one. They did little more than legitimate the Continental Congress. Under them the powers of the Confederation were to be exercised by its Congress; its only executive or judicial organs were to be mere committees or agencies of the Congress; and it was in fact to have no real use for executive parts, for it was to have no executive rights. Its function was to be advice, not command. It hung upon the will of the states, being permitted no effective will of its own. The Articles were scarcely more than an international convention.

35. **The Articles of Confederation** formally vested the exercise of federal functions in a Congress just such as the Continental Congresses had been, — a Congress, that is, consisting of delegates from the several states, and in whose decisions the states were to have an absolutely equal voice. No state, it was arranged, should have her vote in the Congress unless represented by at least two delegates, and no state, on the other hand, was to be entitled to send more than seven delegates; whether she sent two or seven, however, her vote was to be single vote, upon which her delegates were to agree. The government thus constituted was officially known as "The United States in Congress assembled." For the exercise of representative functions it was very liberally and completely equipped. To it the independence of the several states in dealing with foreign powers was entirely subordinated. It alone was to conduct all international correspondence and sanction all international agreements; it was to control the army and navy of the Confederation; it was to preside over federal finances, doing all borrowing and all spending that might be necessary for the purposes of the common government; it was to determine the value of current coin and the standards of weights and measures; it was to be arbitrator in disputes between the states; in brief, it was to be the single and dominant authority for all the graver common interests of the constituent states: its representative position was eminent and complete.

36. **Weakness of the Confederation.** — But it was given absolutely no executive power, and was therefore helpless and contemptible. It could take no important resolution without the difficult concurrence of nine states, — a concurrence made all the more difficult by the fact that the removal of the pressure of the war with England very greatly abated the interest of the states in the functions of the central Con-

gress, and led some of them again and again to fail to send delegates to its sessions; its chief executive agency was a committee of its members representing all the states (hence called the "Committee of States") and bound by the same hard rule of obtaining the concurrence of nine of its thirteen members to every important executive step; and, above all, its only power to govern the states was a power to advise them. It could ask the states for money, but it could not compel them to give it; it could ask them for troops, but could not force them to heed the requisition; it could make treaties, but must trust the states to fulfil them; it could contract debts, but must rely upon the states to pay. them. It was a body richly enough endowed with prerogatives, but not at all endowed with powers. "The United States in Congress assembled" formed a mere consultative and advisory board.

37. **Need of a Better Union.** — It was the fatal executive impotency of the Confederation which led to the formation of the present stronger and more complete government. The old Continental Congresses had sufficed, after a fashion, to keep the colonies together so long as the pressure of the war continued; throughout that war there had been, despite much indifference now and again on the part of some of the colonies to their duty, and of not a little positive dereliction of plain obligations, a wonderful degree of energy and unity of action among the confederated colonists. But when the pressure of the war was removed there was an ominous access of indifference, an ill-boding decrease of respect for plighted faith between the states. Signs fast multiplied both of the individual weakness of the states and of the growth of threatening jealousies between them. A war of tariffs began between neighbor states on the seaboard, notably between New York and New Jersey and between Virginia and Maryland. In Massachusetts there flared out, by reason of the poverty engendered by the war, a rebellion of debtors under Daniel Shays which it was for a moment feared the state authorities might find it hard to cope with. It speedily became evident that, both for the sake of internal order and of inter-state peace and goodwill, a real central government was needed. Central consultation would not suffice;

there must be central government.   The Confederation, therefore, was no real advance upon the old Continental Congresses.
Before a single decade had passed over the new government
with its fair-spoken Articles a new union had been erected and .
the real history of the United States begun.

38.   **The Constitution: Colonial Precedents.** — The present Constitution erects a very different government: it is the
charter of a federal state, which has a commanding law and an
independent power of its own, whose Constitution and law are
the supreme law of the land.   The Convention which framed
the new constitution met in Philadelphia in May, 1787, and
fused together over the slow fires of prolonged debate the elements of English and colonial precedent which were to constitute the government of the United States.   In the debates of
that Convention during that memorable summer are to be read
the particulars of the translation of English precedent into
American practice made during the formative colonial period.
Through the instrumentality of the able men who composed
that extraordinary assembly, the government of the United
States was fitted out with the full experience of the colonies
and of the revolutionary states.[1]   It was arranged that the
legislature of the new federal government should consist of
two houses, not in direct imitation of the English system,
whose House of Lords we did not, of course, have the mate-
rials for reproducing, but in conformity with an almost universal example set by the states.   A single state furnished the
precedent in accordance with which a real difference of character was given to the two houses.   The upper house of the
Connecticut legislature was constituted by an equal represen-

[1] In describing the work of the Convention I follow here Professor
Alexander Johnston's clear exposition given in the *New Princeton Review*
for September, 1887, under the title "The First Century of the Constitution."   A convenient brief survey of the chief features of the state
constitutions at the time of the formation of the present government of the
Union may be found in Hildreth, Vol. III., Chap. XLIV.

tation of the towns of the state, while her lower house represented her people at large : and Connecticut's example showed the Convention a convenient way of compromise by which they could reconcile the two parties within it which were contending, the one for an equal representation of the states in Congress after the absolute manner of the Confederation, the other for a proportional representation of the people simply. The Senate, it was agreed, should represent the states equally, the House of Representatives the people proportionally. The names Senate and House of Representatives were to be found already in use by several of the States. The single Executive, the President, was an obvious copy of the state governors, many of whom at that time bore the name of president; his veto power was to be found formulated ready to hand in the constitution of New York : a method of impeachment was already prepared in the constitutions of half a dozen states. Several states had also the office of Vice-President. With a fine insight into the real character of the government which they were constructing, the Convention provided that its judiciary should be placed, not under the President or the houses, but alongside of them, upon a footing of perfect equality with them, and that with it, as a co-ordinate branch of the government, should rest the weighty prerogative of passing upon the constitutionality of all laws. A similar arrangement obtained under the state constitutions, but the function of constitutional interpretation was necessarily as old as written charters and constitutions, had been an inevitable corollary to their fundamental proposition of a gift of limited powers. Written constituent law is by its very nature a law higher than the legislature acting under it can enact, and by that law, as by an invariable standard, must the courts test all acts of legislation.[1] The colonial courts had often upon this principle questioned the validity of colonial legislation, and the Supreme Court of

[1] See A. V. Dicey, *The Law of the Constitution*, Chap. III.; and J. Bryce, *The American Commonwealth*, Chap. XXIII.

the United States had long had a prototype in the Judicial Committee of the Privy Council, whose function it was to hear appeals from the colonies, and whose practice it had been to pronounce against all laws incompatible with the royal charters.

39. When they came to equip Congress with powers, the Convention adopted the plan of careful enumeration : it set out the acts of government which were to be permitted to the legislature of the new government in a distinctly cast list of eighteen items. Even in doing this, however, they may be said to have been simply recording the experience of the Confederation : they were giving Congress, the powers for lack of which the Congress of the Confederation had proved helpless and ridiculous. It was only when they came to construct the machinery for the election of the President that they left the field of American experience and English example and devised an arrangement which was so original that it was destined to break down almost as soon as it was put in operation.

40. This general statement of the broader features of the selective work of the Convention will suffice for the present : other more particular references to state precedent and experience may be made in their proper connections in our further discussion of the government. I wish in these paragraphs only to fix the attention of the student, by way of clarifying preparation, upon the instructive fact that the work of the Convention was a work of selection, not a work of creation, and that the success of their work was not a success of invention, always most dangerous in government, but a success of judgment, of selective wisdom, of practical sagacity, — the only sort of success in politics which can ever be made permanent.

41. Character of the New Government. — It is one of the distinguishing characteristics of the English race whose political habit has been transmitted to us through the sagacious generation by whom this government was erected that they have never felt themselves bound by the logic of laws, but only by a practical understanding of them based upon slow precedent. For this race the law under which they live is at

any particular time *what it is then understood to be;* and this understanding of it is compounded of the circumstances of the case. Absolute theories of legal consequence they have never cared to follow out to their conclusions. Their laws have always been used as parts of the practical running machinery of their politics, — parts to be fitted from time to time, by interpretation, to existing opinion and social condition.

42. **Character of the Government Changes with Opinion.** — It requires a steady, clear-viewed, thoroughly informed historical sense, therefore, to determine what was at any given time the real character of our political institutions. To us of the present day it seems that the Constitution framed in 1787 gave birth in 1789 to a national government such as that which now constitutes an indestructible bond of union for the states; but the men of that time would certainly have laughed at any such idea, — and for the English race, as I have said, every law is what those who administer it think that it is. The men of 1789 meant to form "a more perfect union" than that which had existed under the Confederation: they saw that for the colonies there must be union or disintegration; they thought union needful and they meant to have it in any necessary degree. But they had no special love for the union which they set about consummating, and they meant to have as little of it as possible, — as little as might be compatible with wise providence as to the welfare of the new-fledged states. They were even more afraid of having too strong a central government than of having one which was too weak, and they accepted the new constitution offered them by the Convention of 1787 because convinced of the truth of the arguments urged by its friends to the effect that the union would be federal merely and would involve no real sacrifice of individuality or autonomy on the part of the states.

43. **Early Sentiment towards the Union.** — It is astonishing to us of this generation to learn how much both of hostility and of indifference was felt for the new government,

which we see to have been the salvation of the country. Even those who helped make it and who worked most sincerely for its adoption entertained grave doubts as to its durability; some of them even questioned, in despondent moments, its usefulness. Philosophic statesmen like Alexander Hamilton supported it with ardent purpose and sustained hope; but for the average citizen, who was not in the least degree philosophic, it was at first an object of quite unexciting contemplation. It was for his state, each man felt, that his blood and treasure had been poured out: it was that Massachusetts and Virginia might be free that the war had been fought, not that the colonies might have a new central government set up over them; patriotism was state patriotism. The states were living, organic persons: the union was an arrangement, — possibly it would prove to be only a temporary arrangement; new adjustments might have to be made.

44. **Early Tolerance for Threats of Secession.** — It is by this frame of mind on the part of the first generation that knew the present constitution that we must explain the undoubted early tolerance for threats of secession. The Union was too young to be sacred; the self-love of the states was too pronounced to be averse from the idea that complete state independence might at any time be resumed. Discontent in any quarter was the signal for significant hints at possible withdrawal. As the new system lived on from year to year and from year to year approved itself strong and effective it became respected; as it gathered dignity and force regard was added to respect, until at last the federal government became a rallying centre for great parties moved by genuine national sentiment. But at first neither love nor respect shielded the federal authorities from the jealousies and menaces of the states. The new government was to *grow* national with the growth of a national history and a national sentiment.

45. **Growth of the National Idea.** — The career and fate of the Federalist Party very well illustrate the first state of

opinion concerning the Union. The Federalist party was the party of the Constitution, — the party which had been chiefly instrumental in bringing about the adoption of the new frame of government. Immediately upon the inauguration of the present Union this party of its friends was put in charge of the new central body politic. It presided over the critical period of its organization, and framed the first measures which gave it financial credit, international consideration, security, and energy. But it soon became evident that the Federalists held views as to the nature of the new government which not all of those who had voted for the adoption of the Constitution were willing to sanction. They assumed for the federal authorities prerogatives of too great absoluteness, and seemed to not a few to be acting upon the idea that the purpose of the Constitution was to subordinate, and if need be sacrifice, state interests to the interests of the general government. Very speedily, therefore, they brought a reaction upon themselves, and were displaced by a party which felt that the limitations put by the Constitution upon federal authority ought to be very strictly observed. This new party, calling itself 'Democratic-Republican,' may be said to have been created by the injudicious excesses of the Federalists; and from this point of view the Federalist party may be said to have effected its own destruction. After its first national defeat it never again came into power. Rapidly in some places, slowly in others, it went utterly to pieces.

46. But, although the Federalist party was destroyed, time worked in favor of its political conceptions. The Democratic-Republicans soon found that success in conducting the affairs of the federal government was, even for them, conditioned upon very liberal readings of the authority conferred by the Constitution; and by slow degrees they drifted into practices of 'broad construction' quite as abhorrent to their own first principles as the much-berated measures of the Federalists had been. But the Democratic-Republicans, — or the Demo-

crats, as they were before long more briefly described, — had the advantage of a corresponding change in public opinion. That, too, was steadily becoming nationalist in its tendencies.

47. Railroads, Expansion, and War aid the National Idea. — So long as the people of one section of the country saw little or nothing of the people of the other sections, separateness of feeling and localness of view continued to exist and to exercise a controlling force; the majority of the people continued to put the states before the nation in their thoughts and to demand more or less punctilious regard for state prerogatives.   But when railroads began to be built and to multiply; when people from all parts of the Union began to go out and settle the West together; when seeing each other and trading with each other began to make the people of all the states very much alike in most of the greater things of habit and institution, and even in most of the smaller things of opinion and conduct; when new states which had grown up in the West without any of the old conservative colonial traditions began to be admitted to the Union in increasing numbers, regarding themselves as born in and of the Union; when a second war with England and a hot struggle with Mexico had tested the government and strengthened a sentiment of national patriotism, — then at length it began to be very generally thought that the Federalists had been right after all; that the federal government ought to come first in consideration, even at the cost of some state pride.

48. Slavery stands in the Way of Nationality. — What stood most in the way of the universal growth of this sort of national feeling was the great difference between the northern and southern portions of the Union caused by the existence of slavery in the South.   So long as the laborers in the South were slaves and those of the North free men, these two sections could not become like one another either socially or politically, and could not have the same national feeling.   The North and Northwest meant one thing when they spoke of the

nation; the South meant quite another thing. Each meant
a nation socially and politically like itself. The two sections,
therefore, rapidly became dissatisfied with living together under
the same political system, and the secession so much talked
about in various quarters in the earlier days of the Union at
last became a reality. Inevitably came the war of secession,
by means of whose fiery processes the differences of institution
between North and South were to be swept utterly away.

49. **Civil War completes the Union.** — The war wrought
changes of the most profound character. Secession was prevented, the Union was preserved, and slavery was forever
abolished; these were the immediate effects of the struggle;
but the remoter results were even more important. They pene-
trated to the changing of the very nature of the Union, though
the form of the federal government remained in all essential
features unaltered. The great effect of the war was, that the
nation was made homogeneous. There was no longer any
permanent reason why the South should not become like the
rest of the country in character and sentiment. Both sections
were brought to the same modes of life and thought; there
was no longer any obstacle to our being in reality one great
nation. The effort made in the war, moreover, to preserve the
Union, and the result of the war in making the country at last
homogeneous throughout, has made the federal government, as
representative of the nation, seem greater in our eyes than
ever before, and has permanently modified in the profoundest
manner the way in which all the old questions concerning
constitutionality and state rights are regarded.

50. **Present Character of the Union.** — It of course by no
means follows that because we have become in the fullest organic sense a nation, ours has become a unitary government,
its federal features merged in a new national organization.
The government of the Union has indeed become permanent,
the cherished representative, the vital organ of our life as a
nation; but the states have not been swallowed up by the fed-

eral power: their prerogatives are as essential to our system as ever, — are indeed becoming more and more essential to it from year to year as the already vastly complex organism of the nation expands.   But, instead of regarding the government of the United States and the government of a state as two governments, as our fathers did, we now regard them, — if we may make a matter-of-fact analysis of our working views in politics, — as two parts of one and the same government, two complementary parts of a single system.   The value of the plan of government which our statesmen adopted at the first, the plan of functions divided between national and state authorities, has abated not a whit: we are only a little less anxious about the clearness of the lines of division.   The national government still has its charter, somewhat enlarged since the war, but substantially the same document as of old; and the national authorities must still confine themselves to measures within the sanction of that charter: the state governments, too, still have their charters, and still have valid claim to all powers not specifically delegated to the government of the Union.   Liberal construction of the federal charter the nation wants, but not a false construction of it.   The nation properly comes before the states in honor and importance, not because it is *more* important than they are, but because it is all-important to them and to the maintenance of every principle of government which we have established and now cherish.   The national government is the organic frame of the states: it has enabled, and still enables, them to exist.

51. **Present Character of the Government of the Union.** — It is perhaps most in accordance with the accomplished results of our national development to describe the government of the United States, not as a dual government, but as a *double* government, so complete is the present integration of its state and federal parts.   Government with us has ceased to be plural and has become singular, the *government* of the United States: distinct as are its parts, they are not separate.   For the sake of

convenience, we speak of the government of the Union and of the government of a state, as if the two were quite separate; but such phraseology scarcely conveys a just impression of the realities of our practice. The state and federal systems are so adjusted under our public law that they may not only operate smoothly and effectively each in the sphere which is exclusively its own, but also fit into each other with perfect harmony of co-operation wherever their jurisdictions cross or are parallel, acting as parts of one and the same frame of government, with an uncontested subordination of functions and an undoubted common aim.

52.   Although these two parts of our government are thus vitally united, however, thus integrated into what is in reality a single scheme of government, state law by no means depends upon federal law for its sanction. The Constitution of the United States and the laws and treaties passed in pursuance thereof are indeed the supreme law of the land, but their supremacy does not trench upon or displace the self-originated authority of the states in the immensely important sphere reserved to them. Although it is true, taking our system as a whole, that the governments of the states are subordinate in our political order to the government of the Union, they are not subordinate in the sense of being subject to be commanded by it, but only in being less than national in their jurisdiction.

53.   **The States not Administrative Divisions but Constituent Members of the Union.** — The common and convenient distinction between central and local government furnishes no ground of discrimination as between the federal and state governments. A central government, as contradistinguished from a local government within the meaning of this distinction, is a government which prescribes both the constitution and the mode of action of the lesser organs of the system to which it belongs. This the governments of the states do with reference to the townships, the counties, the cities within their territories: these local bodies are merely administrative divis-

ions of the states, agencies delegated to do the daily work of government. But, of course, there is no such relationship between the federal government and the states. They are not administrative divisions but constituent members of the Union, co-ordinate with the Union in their powers, in no sense subject to it in their appropriate spheres. They are excluded, indeed, by the federal Constitution from the exercise of certain functions, but the great and all-important functions which they do exercise are not given them by that Constitution: they are exercised, on the contrary, upon the completest principles of self-direction. We may properly distinguish the government of a county and the government of a state by the distinction between local and central government, but not the government of a state and the government of the Union.

CHARACTER, ORGANS, AND FUNCTIONS OF THE STATES.

54. **The States** properly come first in a description of the government of this country, not only because it was in conformity with state models and precedents that the federal government was constructed, but also and more particularly because the great bulk of the business of government still rests with the state authorities; because the states still carry by far the greater part of the weight of the governing function, still constitute the ordinary fountains of justice and of legal right, still stand nearest the people in the regulation of all their social and legal relationships. Like the Swiss Cantons (sec.* 515). our states have given to the government which binds them together their own forms of constitution; but even more than the Cantons have our states retained their right to rule their citizens in all ordinary matters without federal interference. They are the chief creators of law among us. They are the chief constituent units of our political system not only, but are also self-directive units. They make up the mass, the body, the constituent tissue, the organic stuff of the government of

the country. To them is intrusted our daily welfare, to the federal government only our collective interests. Upon the character of the state governments depends the character of the nation in its several constituent members; upon the character of the federal government depends the character of the nation as a whole. If we are to begin our study of our institutions at the centre, the heart of self-government, we must begin with the states.

55. The Law of the States: Its Character. — The law of each state consists of two great parts, (1) the Constitution, statutes, and treaties of the United States and (2) the constitution and statutes of the state. The Constitution, statutes, and treaties of the United States are the supreme law of the land not so much in the sense of being set above the constitutions and laws of the states as in the sense of being, by virtue of the principles of our public law, integral parts of the law of the states. The constitutions of several of the states declare the Constitution of the United States to be a part of the fundamental law of those states: but such declarations are only formal recognitions of a principle now indubitable. On their legal as well as on their political side the two parts of our system have been completely integrated. Upon the state courts as well as upon the courts of the United States rests the duty of administering federal law. The federal Constitution is a negative portion of state law in respect of the limitations which it sets to the sphere of state activity; but the laws passed by Congress under the authority of that Constitution are also positive portions of state law, whose mandates all officers of government, whether state or federal, are bound to observe.

56. The constituted authorities of the states do not stand in the same relation, however, to the Constitution and laws of the Union that they bear to state law: of state law they are the final interpreters, but of federal law they are only provisional interpreters. In acting upon federal law state officers always act subject to the supervision of the federal tribunals.

57. The functions of the state courts with regard to the interpretation of federal law very forcibly illustrate the adjustments of our system.   If in any case brought in a state court the question arise whether a certain state law involved in the case is or is not in violation of the Constitution of the United States, the court may freely give its judgment upon the question, and if its judgment be that the law is *not* constitutional that judgment is conclusive : only when it declares the law to be in agreement with the federal Constitution may its opinion be cited to a federal tribunal for revision.   The federal law is, thus, not regarded as a thing apart from the law of a state, too sacred to be handled by any but the federal courts, its specially constituted guardians : it is a part of state law and the state courts may declare and apply its principles.   But of course in the last resort the federal courts are themselves to shield it from a too liberal or too prejudiced judgment by state judges, who may very conceivably be interested to vindicate the statutes of their state as against any objections drawn from the law of the Union.   Both for the sake of making it uniform and for the sake of keeping it supreme must federal law receive its final adjudication in its own courts.

58.   Scope of State Law. — A moment's thought suffices to reveal how very great a field of activity, how preponderant a part remains under our system to the states.   The powers of the federal government seem great by enumeration : besides being intrinsically powers of the greatest importance, they are made the more imposing in the Constitution by the fact of their being set forth in an exhaustive list.   The *residuum* of powers that remains to the states, consisting as it does of un-enumerated items, is of course vague, and because vague seems unimportant by comparison.   A moment's examination of this *residuum* however, a moment's consideration of its contents, puts a very different face on the matter.   It is worth while for the sake of an adequate understanding of the real division of powers under our government to give to the powers remaining with the states something like the same setting forth that is given to those granted to the Union.

59.   Legislative Powers of the Union. — The Constitution of the United States grants to Congress first of all, of course, the power to lay and collect taxes, duties, imposts, and excises for the support of the government of the Union, the payment of its debts, and the promotion of the common defence and welfare, and also the power to borrow money on the credit of the United States; but these powers of taxation and borrowing belong also to the states, except that they must raise their revenues without resort to duties, imposts, and excises, the privilege of imposing these being reserved to the Union exclusively. The powers which distinguish the general government from the governments of the states are not these powers of raising money but these others: To control the monetary system of the country, to maintain post-offices and post-roads, to grant patents and copyrights, to deal with crimes committed on the high seas or against the law of nations, to shape the foreign relations of the country, to declare war and control the military forces of the nation, and to regulate commerce both with foreign countries and among the states. It is empowered also to establish uniform rules of naturalization and uniform laws concerning bankruptcy; but these powers do not belong to it exclusively; in case Congress does not act in these matters, the states may adopt laws for themselves concerning them. All the powers of the general government are plainly such as affect interests which it would be impossible to regulate harmoniously by any scheme of separate state action, and only such; all other powers whatever remain with the states.

60. **Powers withheld from the States.** —Some powers the Constitution of the United States expressly withholds from the states, besides those granted exclusively to the general government: No state may pass any bill of attainder, *ex post facto* law, or law impairing the obligation of contracts, or grant any title of nobility; no state may, without the consent of Congress, lay any imposts or duties, keep troops or ships of war in time of peace, enter into any agreement with another state or with a foreign power, or engage in war unless actually invaded or in such immediate danger as will not admit of delay. But

these prohibitions obviously curtail scarcely at all the sphere
which the states would in any case normally occupy within
the scheme of federal union.

61. **Powers left with the States.** — Compared with the
vast prerogatives of the state legislatures, these limitations
seem small enough. All the civil and religious rights of our
citizens depend upon state legislation; the education of the
people is in the care of the states; with them rests the regulation of the suffrage; they prescribe the rules of marriage, the
legal relations of husband and wife, of parent and child; they
determine the powers of masters over servants and the whole
law of principal and agent, which is so vital a matter in all
business transactions; they regulate partnership, debt and
credit, insurance; they constitute all corporations, both private
and municipal, except such as specially fulfil the financial or
other specific functions of the federal government; they control the possession, distribution, and use of property, the exercise of trades, and all contract relations; and they formulate
and administer all criminal law, except only that which con-
cerns crimes committed against the United States, on the high
seas, or against the law of nations. Space would fail in which
to enumerate the particulars of this vast range of power; to
detail its parts would be to catalogue all social and business
relationships, to examine all the foundations of law and order.

62. A striking illustration of the preponderant part played by state
law under our system is supplied in the surprising fact that only one
out of the dozen greatest subjects of legislation which have engaged
the public mind in England during the present century would have come
within the powers of the federal government under the Constitution as
it stood before the war, only two under the Constitution as it stands
since the addition of the war amendments. I suppose that I am justi-
fied in singling out as these twelve greatest subjects of legislation the
following: Catholic emancipation, parliamentary reform, the abolition
of slavery, the amendment of the poor-laws, the reform of municipal
corporations, the repeal of the corn laws, the admission of the Jews to
Parliament, the disestablishment of the Irish church, the alteration of

the Irish land laws, the establishment of national education, the introduction of the ballot, and the reform of the criminal law. Of these every one except the corn laws and the abolition of slavery would have been under our system, so far as they could be dealt with at all, subjects for state regulation entirely; and of course it was only by constitutional amendment made in recognition of the accomplished facts of the war that slavery, which was formerly a question reserved for state action, and for state action alone, was brought within the field of the federal authority.[1]

63. **Non-constitutional Provisions in State Constitutions.** —One of the most characteristic features of our state law is the threatened loss of all real distinction between constitutional and ordinary law. Constitutions are of course advertised by their name to be bodies of law by which government is *constituted*, by which, that is, government is given its organization and functions. Private law, the regulation of the relations of citizens to each other in their private capacities, does not fall within their legitimate province. This principle is fully recognized in the construction of our federal Constitution, which is strong and flexible chiefly because of its great, its admirable simplicity and its strictly *constitutional* scope. But constitution-making in the states, especially in the newer states, has proceeded upon no such idea. Not only do the constitutions of the states go very much more into detail in their prescriptions touching the organization of the government; they go far beyond organic provisions and undertake the ordinary, but very different, work of legislative enactment. They commonly embody regulations, for example, with reference to the management of state property, such as canals and roads, and for the detailed administration of the state debt; they determine the amounts and sorts of property which are to be exempt from seizure for private debt; they formulate sumptuary laws, such as those forbidding the sale of intoxicating liquors; at a score of points they enter without hesitation

[1] See J. F. Jameson, *Introduction to the Constitutional and Political History of the Individual States*, Johns Hopkins Univ. Studies in Hist. and Pol. Sci., Fourth Series, p. 9 (continuous p. 189).

or misgiving the field usually reserved for the action of legislative bodies.

64. **Distrust of Legislation.** — The motive, of course, is dissatisfaction with legislation, distrust of legislators, a wish to secure for certain classes of law a greater permanency and stability than is vouchsafed to statutes, which stand in constant peril of repeal. A further motive is the desire to give to such laws the sanction of a popular vote. The practice has its analogies to the Swiss *Referendum* (secs.* 521, 557). It is the almost universal practice throughout the Union to submit constitutional provisions to a vote of the people; and the non-constitutional provisions which are becoming so common in our constitutions are virtually only ordinary laws submitted to popular sanction and so placed, along with the rest of the instrument of which they form incongruous parts, beyond the liability of being changed otherwise than through the acquiescence of the same ultimate authority. The practice perhaps discovers a tendency towards devising means for making all very important legal provisions dependent upon direct popular participation in the act of enactment.

65. **The objections to the practice** are as obvious as they are weighty. General outlines of organization, such as the Constitution of the United States contains, may be made to stand without essential alteration for long periods together; but in proportion as constitutions make provision for interests whose aspects must change from time to time with changing circumstance, they enter the domain of such law as must be subject to constant modification and adaptation. Not only must the distinctions between constitutional and ordinary law hitherto recognized and valued tend to be fatally obscured, but the much to be desired stability of constitutional provisions must in great part be sacrificed. Those constitutions which contain the largest amount of extraneous matter, which does not concern at all the structure or functions of government, but only private or particular interests, must of course, however carefully drawn, prove subject to most frequent change. In some of our states, accordingly, constitutions have been as often changed as important statutes. The danger is that constitution-making will become with us only a cumbrous mode of legislation.

66.   In one or two of the States the Swiss *Referendum* has been more exactly reproduced, though not, so far as I know, in conscious imitation of Swiss example. Thus the Wisconsin constitution leaves it with the people to decide whether banks shall be established by state law or not; and the constitution of Minnesota makes certain railway laws and all appropriations from the internal improvement land fund of the State dependent for their validity upon the sanction of a popular vote.

> The objections to the *referendum* are, of course, that it assumes a discriminating judgment and a fulness of information on the part of the people touching questions of public policy which they do not often possess, and that it lowers the sense of responsibility on the part of legislators.

67.   Constitutional **Amendments.** — The amendment of state constitutions, like the amendment of the federal constitution, can be effected only by elaborate, formal, and unusual processes which are meant to hedge the fundamental law about with a greater dignity and sanctity than attaches to any other body of legal precepts. The theory of our whole constitutional arrangement is, that the people have not only, in establishing their constitutions, bound their agents, the governing bodies and officials of the states, but have also bound themselves, — have bound themselves to change the fundamental rules which they have made only by certain formal and deliberate processes which must mark the act of change as at once solemn and fully advised.

> 68.   **In England,** as we have seen (sec.* 730), constitutional amendment is not distinguishable from simple legislation. Parliament may, by simple Act, change any, even the most fundamental, principle of government that the deliberate opinion of the nation wishes to see changed. Where the constitution consists for the most part of mere precedent, and for the rest of Acts of Parliament or royal ordinances simply, it may be altered as easily as precedent may be departed from. In England that is not easily. The great conservative force there is the difficulty with which Englishmen abandon established courses. **In**

France, constitutional amendment differs from ordinary legislation only in this, that the two chambers must sit together at Versailles, as a single National Assembly, when passing laws which affect the constitution (sec.* 318). *In Germany* constitutional amendment differs from ordinary legislation only in the number of votes required for the passage of an amendment through the *Bundesrath*, in which fourteen negative votes will defeat it (secs.* 404, 406, n.). In the United States, on the contrary, constitutional amendment differs from ordinary legislation both in formal procedure and in the political powers called into action to effect it. The people have always a voice.

69. **Preliminary Steps of Amendment.** — Legislatures, with us, may not undertake any general revision of the fundamental law. In case a general revision of a state constitution is sought to be effected, the legislature is empowered to propose the calling of a popular convention to be chosen specially for the purpose; the question whether or not such a convention shall be called must be submitted to the people; if they vote for its being summoned, it is elected by the usual suffrage; it meets and undertakes the revision, and then submits the results of its labors to the popular vote, which may either accept those results, or reject them and fall back upon the old constitutional arrangements.

> In very many states a proposition for the calling of such a convention may be submitted to the people only if adopted by a two-thirds vote of both houses of the legislature.

70. **Proposal of Amendments.** — Legislatures may, however, themselves propose particular amendments to constitutional provisions. In some of the states a mere majority vote suffices for the preliminary adoption of amendments by the legislature, though in most larger majorities, ranging from three-fifths of a quorum to two-thirds of the elected members of each house, must be obtained. But in almost all cases popular sanction must follow: a vote of the people being made an indispensable condition precedent to the incorporation of an amendment in the fundamental law. In many states, in-

deed, amendments proposed thus by the legislature must be adopted by two *successive* legislatures besides receiving the people's sanction before it can become part of the constitution; in some a popular vote intervenes between the two legislative adoptions which must be had before the desired amendment is effected.

71. Of course the details of these processes differ widely in different states. In Vermont only the senate can propose amendments, and it only at intervals of ten years. In Connecticut amendments can be originated only by the house of representatives. Various restrictions, too, are in many of the states put upon the number of clauses of the constitution to which amendments can be proposed at any single legislative session, the number of times amendments may be submitted to the people within a specified term of years, and the method to be followed in the popular vote when more than one amendment is submitted. In most states, too, special popular majorities are required for the adoption of all constitutional changes.

72. These processes of amendment have been found by no means so difficult as they seem. The habit of inserting in state constitutions enactments not properly belonging with constitutional provisions, and which must be subject to frequent alteration, has of course led to frequent appeals to the people for purposes of amendment, and has served to show how easy amendment may be made. So easy and normal, indeed, have appeals to the people in state affairs become that the constitution of New Hampshire goes to the length of providing for the submission to the vote of the people every seven years of the question whether or not the state constitution shall be revised by a convention called for the purpose, while that of Iowa commands the submission of the same question to the people every ten years, that of Michigan every sixteen years; and the constitutions of New York, Ohio, Virginia, and Maryland direct its submission every twenty years.

73. **Conflict of Laws.** — This plan of leaving to the states the regulation of all that portion of the law which most nearly touches our daily interests, and which in effect determines the whole structure of society, the whole organic action of industry and business, has some very serious disadvantages: disadvantages which make themselves more and more em-

phatically felt as modern tendencies of social and political
development more and more prevail over the old conservative
forces. When the Constitution of the Union was framed the
states were practically very far distant from one another. Dif-
ficulties of travel very greatly restricted intercourse between
them : being, so to say, physically separate, it was no inconvenience that they were also legally separate. But now that
the railroad and the telegraph have made the country small
both to the traveller and to the sender of messages the states
have been in a sense both geographically and socially fused.
Above all, they have been commercially fused, industrially
knit together; state divisions, it turns out, are not natural
economic divisions; they practically constitute no boundaries
at all to any distinctly marked industrial regions. Variety
and conflict of laws, consequently, have brought not a little
friction and confusion alike into our social and into our business arrangements.

74. **Detrimental Effects.** — At some points this diversity
and multiformity of law almost fatally affects the deepest and
most abiding interests of the national life. Above all things
else, it has touched the marriage relation, that tap-root of all
social growth, with a deadly corruption. Not only has the
marriage tie been very greatly relaxed in some of the states,
while in others it retains its old-time tightness, so that the
conservative rules which jealously guarded the family, as the
heart of the state, promise amid the confusion to be almost
forgotten; but diversities between state and state have made
possible the most scandalous processes of collusive divorce and
fraudulent marriage.

It has become possible for either party to a marriage to go into
another state and, without acquiring there even a legal residence, obtain
from its courts a routine divorce because the other party has not
answered a summons to defence published only in the state in which
suit is instituted for divorce and therefore practically certain not to be
brought to the notice of the person for whom it is intended.

Under such a system a person may be divorced without knowing it, and it may be possible for a man to keep different wives, or a woman different husbands, in several states at the same time.

75. **In the matter of taxation** so great a variety of law obtains among the states as to preclude in part a normal and healthy economic development: special taxes drive out certain employments from some states, special exemptions artificially foster them in others; and in many quarters ill-judged or ill-adjusted systems of taxation tend to hamper industry and exclude capital. So, too, as to corporations diversity of state law works great confusion and partial disaster to the interests of commerce, not only because some states are less careful in their creation and control of corporations than others, and so work harm to their own citizens, but also because loosely incorporated companies created by the laws of one state may do business and escape proper responsibility in another state.

76. **In the criminal law,** again, variety works social damage, tending to concentrate crime where laws are lax, and to undermine by diffused percolation the very principles which social experience has established for the control of the vicious classes. So, too, in laws concerning debt, special exemptions or special embarrassments of procedure here, there, and everywhere impair that delicate instrument, credit, upon whose perfect operation the prosperity of a commercial nation depends.

77. **Bankruptcy.** — One of the most serious legal embarrassments at the present time (1888) is the lack of a national bankrupt law. Since the repeal of the bankrupt law of 1867 (1878) Congress has neglected to exercise its constitutional right to legislate on the subject of bankruptcy. The consequence is that, in the absence of any action in the matter by the states, the relations of debtor and creditor have fallen into dire confusion. This is due, however, to no fault of the system, of course, but only to the neglect of Congress.

78. **Proposals of Reform.** — It is in view of such a state of affairs, such a multiformity and complexity of law touching matters which ought, for the good of the country, to be uni-

formly and simply regulated throughout the Union, that various extensions of the sphere of the federal government have
been proposed by sanguine reformers, who would have all interests which need for their advancement uniform rules of law
given over to the care of Congress by constitutional amendment.

79. **Evils of the Case easily exaggerated.** — Of course the
extent of the legal friction and confusion complained of may
easily be exaggerated. It is in most cases a confusion of detail
and of procedure rather than of principle or substance, and has
more exasperations for the lawyer than for the layman. Unquestionably there is vastly more uniformity than diversity.
All the states, as I have said, have built up their law upon the
ancient and common foundation of the Common Law of England, the new states borrowing their legislation in great part
from the old. Nothing could afford clearer evidence of this
than the freedom with which, in the courts of nearly every
state in the Union, the decisions of the courts of the other
states, and even the decisions of the English courts, are cited
as suggestive or illustrative, sometimes also as authoritative,
precedent. Everywhere, for instance, the laws of property
rest upon the same bases of legal principle, and everywhere
those laws have been similarly freed from the burdens and inequalities of the older system from which they have been
derived. Everywhere there is the same facility of transfer,
the same virtual abolition of all the feudal characteristics of
tenure, the same separation between the property interests of
man and wife, the same general rules as to liens and other
claims on property, the same principles of tenancy, of disposition by will, of intestate inheritance, and of dower. Everywhere, too, contracts, common carriage, sales, negotiable paper,
partnership, rest upon similar principles of practically universal recognition. We feel the conflicts, because we suffer
under their vexations; while we fail to realize and appreciate
the uniformities because they are normal and have come to
seem matters of course. It must be acknowledged, moreover,

that even within the area of irritation there are strong corrective forces at work, a growing moral sentiment and a healthy fashion of imitation, promising the initiation and propagation of reform. As the country grows socially and politically, its tendency is to compact, to have a common thought and common practices: as it compacts, likenesses will be emphasized, diversities pared and worn away.

    80. **Louisiana**, among the states, and New Mexico, among the territories, stand apart with a peculiar law of their own, unlike the law of the rest of the states, because based upon the civil law of France and Spain, which is Roman law filtered through the histories of the Romance nations. Inevitably, however, the laws of these exceptional states have approximated in some degree to the legal systems of the rest of the Union; and they will draw still closer to them in the future.

    81. **Inter-state Law: Commerce.** — In a country being thus compacted, thus made broader than its states in its feelings and interests, thus turned away from the merely local enterprise of its early industrial history to the national commerce and production of the present generation, state lines must coincide with the lines of very few affairs which are not political: there must be many calls for the adjusting weight of an authority larger than that of any single state. Most such interests, happily, are commercial in their nature, and with the regulation of inter-state commerce Congress has always been charged. It was to give Congress this power, indeed, that the great constitutional convention was called: inter-state commerce was one of the chief sources of the alarming friction between the states which marked that time of crisis. It is by the operation of this power that the great railroad systems of the country, and the endless telegraph lines, have come under the guardianship, and, so far as Congress has chosen, under the regulation of the federal government. Federal law cannot touch agencies of commerce which lie wholly within a single state; but there are nowadays very few such agencies, and the jurisdiction of Congress over commerce,

where it does exist, is exclusive of all interference by the states. Federal law controls all navigable waters which constitute natural highways of inter-state traffic or intercourse, whether directly or only through their connections; it extends to such waters, not only, but also to the control of the means by which commerce must cross them in its land passage, to the construction, that is, of bridges over navigable waters for the facilitation of land traffic. It excludes every state tax or license law, every state regulation whatever, that in any way affects by way of restriction or control any movement of commerce or intercourse between the states.

82. **Posts and Telegraphs.** — Directly supplementary to the power of Congress over inter-state commerce is its power to establish post-offices and post-roads. This has been interpreted to bestow upon Congress the right to facilitate telegraphic intercourse between the states by taking measures to break down exclusive privileges granted by a state; and it must undoubtedly be taken as rounding out to a perfect wholeness the control of the general government over the means of communication between state and state.

83. Of course, too, this is a jurisdiction which must necessarily advance with lengthening strides as the movements of our already vast commerce become yearly even wider still and more rapid. It has been made, indeed, to carry also a promise even of federal ownership of the telegraph system of the country, and of a very much more extensive regulation of railway management than has yet been ventured upon. The most significant step yet taken was, of course, the creation, in 1887, of an Inter-state Commerce Commission charged with the prevention of unjust discriminations in railroad rates either for freight or passage. This Commission has already become one of the most important judicial bodies of the nation, and illustrates a very important experiment in federal control (sec. 288).

84. **Citizenship.** — Citizenship in the United States illustrates the double character of the government. Whoever possesses citizenship in this country is a citizen both of the United States and of the state in which he lives. He cannot

be a citizen of the United States alone, or only of a state; he must be a citizen of both or of neither: the two parts of his citizenship cannot be separated. The responsibilities of citizenship, too, are both double and direct. Under our federal system punishment for the violation of federal law falls directly upon individuals, as does punishment for the violation of state law; the obligation of obedience is in both cases direct: every citizen must obey both federal law and the law of his own state. His citizenship involves direct relations with the authorities of both parts of the government of the country, and connects him as immediately with the power of the marshals of the United States as with the power of the sheriff of his own county.

85.   The population of the United States is probably less stationary in its residence than the population of any other country in the world, and frequent changes of residence have led to great facilitations of the transfer of citizenship from one state to another. A very brief term of abode in a new home in another state secures the privileges of citizenship there: but in transferring his state citizenship a citizen does not, of course, at all affect his citizenship of the United States. The term of residence required for the acquirement of the privilege of suffrage varies from three months to two years and a half, but is in most cases one year.

86.   **Elements of Confusion.** — A very considerable amount of obscurity, it must be admitted, surrounds the question of citizenship in the United States. The laws of our states have so freely extended to aliens the right to hold property, and even the right to vote after a mere declaration of intention to become naturalized citizens (see sec. 106), — have, in brief, so freely endowed aliens with all the most substantial and distinguishing *privileges* of citizenship, — that it has become extremely difficult to draw any clear line, any distinction not merely formal, between citizens and aliens. Of course if a person not formally naturalized exchanges residence in a state, in which he was allowed the privileges of citizenship, for residence in a state in which those privileges are denied him, he can complain of no injustice or inequality. The Constitution of the United States commands that "the citizens of each state shall be entitled to all privileges and immunities of citizens in the several states"; but only federal law admits to formal citizen-

ship, and only formal citizenship can give to any one, wherever he may go, a right to the privileges and immunities of citizenship. The suffrage in particular is a privilege which each state may grant upon terms of its own choosing, provided only that those terms be not inconsistent with a republican form of government (sec. 106).

87. Naturalization. — Naturalization is the name given to the acquirement of citizenship by an alien. The power to prescribe uniform rules of naturalization rests with Congress alone, by grant of the Constitution. The states cannot make rules of their own in the matter, though they may, singularly and inconsistently enough, admit to the privileges of citizenship on what terms they please (sec. 106). The national naturalization law requires that the person who wishes to become a citizen must apply to a court of law in the state or territory in which he desires to exercise the rights of citizenship for formal papers declaring him a legal citizen; that before receiving such papers he must take oath to be an orderly and loyal citizen and renounce any title of nobility he may have held; and that in order to obtain such papers he must have lived in the United States at least five years, and in the state or territory in which he makes application at least one year; and at least two years before his application he must have declared in court under oath his intention to become a naturalized citizen.

It is not necessary for a person who came into the United States to live three years before coming of age to make such a sworn declaration of his intention to become a citizen. If a man who has made sworn declaration in due form of such intention dies before taking out his papers of naturalization, his widow and minor children may become citizens by merely taking the necessary oath of citizenship at the proper time. The children of persons who become naturalized, if they live in the United States, and are under twenty-one years of age when their parents take the oath of citizenship, become citizens by virtue of the naturalization of their parents.

88. **In Germany and Switzerland,** it will be remembered, the states individually admit to citizenship on their own terms, and state citizenship carries with it federal citizenship (secs.* 437, 526). The European states have not, however, any of the problems of naturaliza-

tion which confront and confound us in the United States. The whole world is not coming to them as it is coming to us.

89. **Citizenship under a Confederation.** — The possession of a national naturalization law is one of the practical political features which distinguish our general government from the government of a mere confederation. The states which compose it are the only 'citizens' of a confederation: for the individual there is no federal citizenship; and the transfer by an individual of his citizenship from one state to another within the confederation is as much a mere matter of international comity as if the states were not bound together by any common law.

90. **Central Governments of the States.** — The governments of the states depend for their structure and powers, of course, entirely upon written fundamental law, upon constitutions adopted by the people at the suggestion of conventions consisting of their representatives, — upon documents which we may call popular charters. It was, as I have said, upon the models and precedents furnished by the governments of the thirteen original states that the federal government was constructed, and this was one of the features copied: the state governments, no less distinctly than the federal government, rest upon fundamental law proceeding from an authority higher than themselves.

91. A very great uniformity of structure is observable among the central governments of the states in all general features. One of the most obvious points of resemblance between them is the complete separation and perfect co-ordination of the three great departments of governmental action, — the legislative, the executive and the judicial; and these are set apart and organized under the state constitutions with a very much greater particularity than characterizes the provisions of the federal constitution.

92. **The State Legislatures: Their Powers.** —The state constitutions supplement the constitution of the Union, providing for the exercise of all powers not bestowed by the federal charter; and the legislatures of the states may be said, in

general terms, to possess all law-making powers not given to Congress. But this is by no means a complete statement of the case. State constitutions contain strict limitations of power no less than does the Constitution of the United States. Some powers there are which are altogether withheld: they cannot under our system be exercised by any existing authority: they have been granted neither to Congress nor to the legislatures of the states. Such, for example, is the power to grant to any person or class of persons exclusive political privileges or immunities, the power to bestow hereditary privileges or honors, and the power to abridge in any way the equal rights to life, liberty, and property which all our state constitutions are careful to set forth in more or less elaborate Bills of Rights. These may safely be said, however, to be powers which no state legislature would dream of exercising, inasmuch as they would have to be exercised, if exercised at all, in the face of a public opinion which would certainly refuse re-election to any legislator who should violate the principles of republican government so strenuously worked out in our history, from Magna Charta down, and now so warmly cherished by all classes of our people that no denial of them could stand upon our statute books a single twelvemonth. These are merely limitations put upon reaction.

93. **Limitations of Length of Session, etc.** — There are other limitations, however, of a very different character contained in our state constitutions: limitations meant specially to control the action of legislatures within the sphere of their proper and undoubted powers, and unquestionably based upon a general distrust of the wisdom, if not of the honesty, of legislators. Thus our constitutions very commonly forbid all private or special legislation, confining legislatures to the passage of general laws applying uniform rules to all persons and all cases alike. They limit, moreover, in very many cases, the length and frequency of legislative sessions, providing that the legislature shall convene, for instance, only once in

⁻every period of two years, and shall continue its biennial session for not more than a certain number of days, except under
special or exceptional conditions, when extra sessions may be
called by the governor or regular sessions extended by a special
two-thirds or three-fifths vote. Many constitutions contain,
also, minute provisions concerning the conduct of legislation,
forbidding the introduction of bills later than such and such a
day of a limited session, prescribing the general form of bills,
limiting their subject-matter to a single object each, and even
commanding the manner of their consideration.

94. **Other Limitations.** — More than this, as we have seen,
there are certain classes of legislative provisions which have
been removed beyond the cognizance of legislatures by being
put into the constitutions themselves : such as exemptions of
certain classes of property from seizure for private debt (generally called "Homestead exemptions"), 'prohibition' provis·
ions, etc. The embodiment of such measures in constitutions is,
as I have said (secs. 63, 64), only a means of putting them
beyond legislative interference, — is a limitation of the same
indirect sort as a Bill of Rights. It is usual, also, for our
state constitutions to limit the power of legislatures to create
corporations, by provisions which direct the passage of general
laws of incorporation to be applied in a formal administrative
manner by the courts, to which applications for incorporation
are to be made.

95. The period to which the duration of legislative sessions is restricted varies from forty days (Colorado, Georgia) to ninety days
(Maryland and Virginia), the most usual period being sixty days. It
is noteworthy that only four of the original thirteen states have put a
restriction upon the sessions of their legislatures. Eight of these thirteen have, however, on the other hand, restricted either wholly or in
part the power to pass private or special legislation, — the power, that
is, to make special rules for special cases or for particular individuals.
It is nevertheless true that it is in the newer states, for the most part,
that the strictest and most extensive limitations of legislative power are
to be found.

96. State Legislatures not Sovereign Bodies. — It will thus be seen that our state legislatures are not in any sense 'sovereign' bodies: the only sovereign authority lies with the people. There is a certain serviceable clearness of view to be had by regarding the state governments as corporations: their legislatures are *law-making bodies* acting within the gifts of charters, and by these charters in most cases very strictly circumscribed in their action. It is this fact which gives so unique a place of power under our system to the courts, the authoritative interpreters of the fundamental law to which all legislation and all executive action must conform.

97. Legislative Organization. — In all the states the legislature consists of two houses, a senate and house of representatives, and in most of them the term of senators is four years, that of representatives two years, one-half of the senate being renewed every two years at the general elections. There is no such difference in character, however, between the two houses of the state legislatures as exists between the Senate and the House of Representatives of the United States. Connecticut, as we have seen (sec. 38), furnished the suggestion upon which the framers of the federal constitution acted in deciding upon the basis and character of representation in the two federal houses; for in the Connecticut legislature of that time the senate represented the towns, as the confederate units of the state, while the house represented the people directly. Even Connecticut has now abandoned this arrangement, however, and in almost all the states representation in both houses is based directly upon population, the only difference between the senate and house being that the senate consists of fewer members representing larger districts. Often, for instance, each county of a state is entitled to send several representatives to the lower house of the legislature, while several counties are combined to form a senatorial district.

98. Reasons for Two Houses in State Legislatures. — There is, consequently, no such reason for having two houses in the states as exists in the case of the federal government. The object of the federal arrangement is the representation of the two elements upon which the national government rests, namely, the popular will and a federal union of states. The state legislatures have two houses simply for purposes of deliberateness in legislation, in order, that is, that legislation may be filtered through the debates of two co-ordinate bodies, representing slightly differing constituencies, though coming both directly from the people, and may thus escape the taint of precipitation apt often to attach to the conclusions of a single all-powerful popular chamber. The double organization represents no principle, but only an effort at prudence.

99. The reason for our having double legislatures cannot, however, be so simply explained. It is compounded of both deliberate and historical elements. Its historical grounds are sufficiently clear: the senates of our states are lineal descendants of the councils associated with the colonial governors, though of course they now represent a very different principle. The colonial councils emanated from the executive, and may be said to have been parts of the executive, while our senates, of course, emanate from the people. Then, too, there was the element of deliberate imitation of English institutions. One hundred years ago England possessed the only great free government in the world; she was, moreover, our mother-land, and the statesmen who formed our constitutions at the revolution naturally adopted that English fashion of legislative organization which has since become the prevailing fashion among all liberalized governments. Possibly, too, they were influenced by more ancient example. The two greatest nations of antiquity had had double legislatures, and, because such legislatures existed in ancient as well as in modern times, it was believed that they were the only natural kind.

100. **Historical Precedents.** — Greeks, Romans, and English alike, of course, had at first only a single great law-making body, a great senate representing the elders or nobles of the community, associated with the king, and, because of the power or rank of its members, a guiding authority in the state. In all three nations special historical processes produced at length legislatures representing the people also; the popular assemblies were, on one plan or another, co-ordinated with the aristocratic assembly, and presently the plan of an aristocratic chamber and a popular chamber in close association appeared in full development. We copied the English chambers when they were in this stage of real co-ordination; before her legislature had sustained that great change, which Greece and Rome also had witnessed, whereby all real power came to rest again with a single body, the popular assembly.

101. **Terms of Senators and Representatives.** — Among the older states of the union there is a more noticeable variety of law as to the *terms* of senators and representatives than is to be found on a comparison of the constitutions of the newer states. In Massachusetts and Rhode Island, for instance, the term of both senators and representatives is a single year only. In New Jersey senators are elected for three years, one-third of the senate being renewed every year at the election for representatives, whose term in New Jersey is but one year. A large number of the states, however, both new and old, limit the term of senators to two years, the term of representatives; while in Louisiana representatives are given the same term as senators, namely, four years.

102. **Names of the Houses.** — There is some variety among the states as regards the name by which the lower house of the legislature is known. In New York the popular house is called "the Assembly"; in Virginia, the "House of Delegates"; in New Jersey, the "General Assembly," — a name generally given in most of the states to the two houses taken together.

103. **The qualifications** required of senators and representatives vary widely in the different states, but not in any essential point of principle. It is universally required, for example, that members of the legislature shall be citizens; it is very generally required that they shall be residents of the states, sometimes that they shall be residents of the districts, for which they are elected; and it is in almost all cases required that a member of the legislature shall have reached a certain age. Variety appears in these provisions only in respect of particulars, of details, as to the length of time citizenship or residence shall have been acquired before election, the particular age necessary, etc.

> The age required varies in the case of senators from twenty-one to thirty years, in the case of representatives from twenty-one to twenty-five.

Only in Delaware is a property qualification prescribed. In that state no one can be a senator who is not possessed of a freehold estate of two hundred acres or of personal or mixed estate worth £1000.

104. Legislative Procedure. — The same general rules of organization and procedure are observed in the constitution and business both of Congress and of the state legislatures. The more numerous branch is in all cases presided over by an officer of its own election who is called the 'Speaker'; the senate sits under the presidency, generally, of a *Lieutenant Governor*, who occupies much the same place in the government of the state that the Vice President of the United States occupies in the national government: he is contingent substitute for the governor.

105. Standing Committees. — The houses of the state legislatures, too, being separated from the executive in such a way as to be entirely deprived of its guidance, depend upon standing committees for the preliminary examination, digestion, and preparation of their business, and allow to these committees an almost unquestioned command of the time and the conclusions of the legislature. The state legislatures of the early time, as I have said, served as models for Congress; they and the legislatures of the later states, made like them, have retained substantially that first plan of organization, following the rules of parliamentary practice universally observed among English-speaking peoples; and they and Congress alike have had in the main the same development: as they have grown larger they have grown more dependent upon their advisory parts, their committees.

> In several States the constitutions themselves command the reference of all bills to committees and forbid the passage of any measure which has not been referred and reported upon.

106. The Suffrage. — The suffrage is in all the states given by constitutional provision to male citizens twenty-one years of age; but it does not in all the states stop there. Many of the states extend the privilege of voting also to every male resident of foreign birth who is twenty-one years of age and has declared his intention to become a naturalized citizen;

and ten states grant it to every male citizen or '*inhabitant*' of voting age. The laws of almost all the states require residence in the state for a certain length of time previous to the election in which the privilege is sought to be exercised (the period varies all the way from three months to two years and a half), as a condition precedent to voting; most require a certain length of residence in the county also where the privilege is to be exercised; some a certain length of residence in the voting precinct. Many states require all voters to have paid certain taxes; but no state has a property qualification properly so-called.

107. In Connecticut and Massachusetts the suffrage is confined to those who can read the laws of the state. It is common, of course, throughout the country to exclude criminals, insane persons, idiots, and in several states the privilege is withheld from those who bet on elections. In Florida betting on an election not only excludes from the election in connection with which the offence is committed, but is punished, upon conviction, by entire and permanent disfranchisement. A number of states also shut out duellists.

108. The privilege of voting in school elections is given to women in Massachusetts, Minnesota, and Colorado, though the constitutions of all the states without exception declare the suffrage to be restricted, in general, to males. In the three territories of Washington,[1] Wyoming, and Utah, women are allowed to vote in all elections. In Kansas they have the elective franchise in municipal elections.

109. The State Courts. — A very great variety of course exists among the laws of the several states regarding the constitution, functions, and relative subordination of the courts. A general sketch of the state courts must, therefore, be made in very broad outline. Perhaps in this department of state law, as in others, there may be said to be, despite a bewildering variety of detail, sufficient unity of general feature to warrant a generalized description, and to render unnecessary the unsatisfactory expedient of choosing the institutions of a single

[1] Washington Territory became a state July 1, 1889, being admitted along with Montana, North Dakota, and South Dakota.

state as in some broad sense typical, and describing them alone.

110. The courts of our states are in no sense organs of federal justice, as the courts of the German states are (sec.* 436); they have an entirely independent standing and organization and an entirely independent jurisdiction. Their constitution and procedure are in no way affected by federal law, — except of course by way of limitation; — their sphere is a sphere apart. The series of courts in each state, therefore, is complete: every state has its supreme court, as well as its inferior tribunals, and appeals lie from the state courts to the courts of the United States only in cases involving federal law or in cases where the character of the parties to the suit does not give any state court complete jurisdiction (secs. 57, 250, 251).

111. One of the most characteristic features of our state courts is what I may call their *local attachment*. In most cases the judges are not appointed by any central authority but are elected by the voters of the district or circuit in which they hold court: they, like members of legislatures, may be said to have 'constituents.' Their responsibility is thus chiefly a responsibility to the electors, a popular rather than official responsibility. The courts are held together in a common system and to a common duty *by law*, therefore, not by discipline or official subordination to superior judicial authorities. The courts may be said to be local rather than central organs; they are integrated only by the course of appeal, by the appellate authority of the higher over the lower courts in points of law.

112. This *localization* of the organs of government, in their origin as well as in their functions, is a general characteristic of American political organization, — a characteristic which appears most conspicuously in the arrangements of local government, which is, as we shall see, not so much organized as left to organize itself under general statutes for whose enforcement no central machinery is provided.

113. **Common Law Courts.** — There are, usually, four grades of jurisdiction in the judicial systems of the states, with four grades of courts corresponding.   There are generally (1) *Justices of the Peace*, who have jurisdiction over all petty police offences and over civil suits for trifling sums; who conduct preliminary hearings in cases of grave criminal offence, committing the accused, when there is *prima facie* proof of guilt, for trial by a higher court; and who are, in general terms, conservators of the peace.   They act separately and have quite lost the high judicial estate which still belongs to the English Justices, from whom they take their name.   Their decisions are in almost all cases subject to appeals to higher courts.

> Mayor's courts in the towns are generally the same in rank and jurisdiction, so far as criminal cases are concerned, as the courts of Justices of the Peace.

114. (2) **County or Municipal Courts,** which hear appeals from Justices of the Peace and from Mayor's courts, and whose own original jurisdiction is one step higher than that of the Justices, including civil cases involving considerable sums, and criminal cases generally not of the gravest character.

> Often, however, courts of this grade, especially the municipal courts of the larger towns, are given a much higher jurisdiction and are coordinated in some respects with courts of the next higher grade, the Superior Courts.
>
> In New York, New Jersey, and Kentucky the county courts retain the English name of Quarter Sessions.

115. (3) **Superior Courts,** which hear appeals from the county and municipal courts, and generally from all inferior courts, and which are themselves courts of high original jurisdiction of the most general character in both civil and criminal cases.   They may be said to be the general courts which give to the courts of lower grade their name of 'inferior.'   County and municipal courts, as their names imply, sit only for certain small districts; but the districts over which superior courts have jurisdiction usually cover a wide area, necessitating the

sitting of each such court in several places in succession. In other words, superior courts are generally circuit courts, as in many states they are called.

'Circuit courts' is, indeed, the most generally used name for courts of this grade, that is, for the principal courts of the state; though in almost as many states they are called 'district courts.' In most of the states these courts have, of course, special judges of their own; but in Maine and New Hampshire they are held by the judges of the supreme court on circuit.

116. In some states civil is separated from criminal jurisdiction in this grade, and distinct courts are created for each. Thus in New York there are Circuit courts which hear civil causes and courts of Oyer and Terminer, immediately subordinated to a court of General Sessions, for the hearing of criminal cases; and in Texas there are District courts for civil causes, District Criminal courts for criminal cases. In Pennsylvania courts of Quarter Sessions are the courts of general criminal jurisdiction, as in England, civil causes going to the courts of Common Pleas. Delaware has criminal courts called courts of Gaol Delivery.

117. (4) **Supreme** Courts, which in most of the states have no original jurisdiction at all, but only appellate jurisdiction, hearing appeals in all classes of cases (except such as involve only trifling offences or small sums of money) from the superior courts and from various inferior courts.

118. (5) In five states there are *supremest* courts above the 'supreme.' Thus in New York a Court of Appeals revises errors made in certain cases by the supreme court; in New Jersey there is a supreme court above the circuit, which is itself of high appellate jurisdiction, and a Court of Errors and Appeals above the supreme; in Louisiana the order is reversed and there is a supreme court above a court of appeals; in Illinois a supreme court above certain district "appellate courts"; and in Kentucky a court of appeals above a supreme court which is called 'superior' simply. In Texas there are two co-ordinate supreme courts: one, called the supreme, for the hearing of civil cases only, the other, called the court of appeals, for the hearing of criminal cases and of civil cases brought up from the county courts.

119. Decisions rendered by the supreme court of the District of Columbia are subject to revision by the supreme court of the United States.

120. The name 'court of appeals' is found also in Maryland, Virginia, and West Virginia.

121. In five of the original states (New Hampshire, Massachusetts, Rhode Island, New York, New Jersey), and in Maine, the supreme courts have, anomalously enough, *original* as well as appellate jurisdiction in all cases; but in the newer states such an arrangement is never found.

122. In several of the larger cities of the country there are complete sets of courts, reproducing the state judiciary in small. Thus in Baltimore, for example, there are city courts from the lowest grade up to a "Supreme Bench of Baltimore City."

123. **Courts of Equity.** — "Equity" is defined, under the legal systems of England and the United States, as "that portion of remedial justice which is exclusively administered by a court of equity, as contradistinguished from that portion of remedial justice which is exclusively administered by a court of common law" (Story). In other words, it is that portion of remedial justice which was administered in England by the Chancellors, who were 'the keepers of the king's conscience,' and from whose court, as if from the king's sense of justice, there issued writs from time to time for the remedy of wrongs for which the common law made no adequate provision (secs.* 666, 1189, 1190). The early Chancellors were ecclesiastics imbued with Roman law as it had come down through the medium of the canon law, and both in their hands and in those of their lay successors of later times, who were the heirs of their principles and prerogatives, equity law and procedure became a very different thing from the law and procedure of the common law courts (sec. 125).

124. **Fusion of Law and Equity.** — As time has gone on equity and law have been largely fused, even in England, just as the *jus gentium* and the *jus civile* became merged in the development of the Roman law (secs.* 206, 208, 212, 216); and in most of the states of the Union the same courts exercise both equitable and common law jurisdiction. In several states the whole procedure, even, in both jurisdictions has been made practically identical, and law is not distinguishable from

equity. Generally, however, the distinctive procedure has been preserved, and only courts of the superior and supreme grades have been given equitable jurisdiction, — jurisdiction, that is, over cases in which the remedy is equitable. In Alabama, Delaware, Michigan, Mississippi, New Jersey, Tennessee, and Vermont there are still special chancery courts.

125. Equity processes of trial differ from common law processes, outwardly, chiefly in the fact that the testimony is written instead of oral, and that decisions of fact as well as of law rest with the judge instead of with a jury. For its special subject-matter equity jurisdiction generally embraces such matters as trusts, mistakes, frauds, etc. — matters hardly tangible by ordinary remedies.

126. Probate Courts. — In most of the states there are special probate courts, — special courts, that is, charged with jurisdiction over the proof of wills, the administration of estates, the appointment of guardians, administrators, etc., the care of the estates of wards, and, in general of the proper disposition of the property of persons deceased. In many states, however, these functions are left to the ordinary courts of law.

127. In England this probate jurisdiction was, from the first until a very recent date, a prerogative of the ecclesiastical courts, and in two of our states the probate courts retain the names of the officers who exercised this function in the place of the bishop: in Georgia the court is called the court of the 'Ordinary,' in New York the 'Surrogate's' court. In New Jersey, with a reminiscence of the same origin, it is called the 'Prerogative' court. In several states, on the other hand, it is known, by virtue of one side of its function, as the 'Orphan's' court.

128. Judges. — The judges of most of the state courts are elected, generally by the people, in a few cases by the legislature; only in Delaware are they appointed by the governor, though in several states they are nominated by the governor and appointed by and with the advice and consent of the Senate.

Supreme court judges are usually elected by the people of the state at large; circuit, district, county, municipal, and other judges by the electors of the area in which they serve.

The terms of judges range all the way from two years to a tenure during good behavior.

129. In New Hampshire, Delaware, and Massachusetts all judges of the higher courts hold during good behavior; and in Rhode Island, and the District of Columbia also, judges of the supreme court have a like life tenure.

Of course the length of the term varies with the grade of the court, the tendency being to give longer terms to the judges of the higher courts.

130. **The qualifications** required of judges by state law are not stringent.   Only some eight or nine of the states require by law any identification of their judges with the legal profession; and only six require 'learning in the law'; though of course, custom and public opinion generally confine the choice of judges to professional lawyers.   Generally a certain age is required of judges (varying, where there is such a requirement, from twenty-five to thirty-five years), besides, in most cases, citizenship and residence in the state or circuit.

As a rule single judges hold all the courts except the highest. Supreme courts have a more or less numerous 'bench.'

131. **The ministerial officers of the state courts,** the sheriffs, are generally not appointed by the judges or responsible to them, but elected by the people and answerable to 'constituents,' just as the judges themselves are.   Even the clerks of the courts are often elected.

132. The position of sheriff thus differs very materially from the position of a United States marshal (sec. 259), the sheriff's counterpart in the federal judicial system. The marshal is appointed by the President of the United States, and is responsible to a central authority, is part of a centralized organization of justice. The sheriff, on the contrary, is the organ of an extremely decentralized, an almost disintegrated, organization of justice.

The bailiffs, the sheriff's deputies, are usually the appointees of the sheriff.

133. **The State Executives.** — The Executives of the states are the least distinct parts of state organization, the least sus-

ceptible of being adequately pictured in outline, or indeed in any broad and general way.   Under our system of state law the executive officers of a state government are neither the servants of the legislature, as in Switzerland, nor the responsible guides of the legislature, as in England, nor the real controlling authority in the execution of the laws, as under our own federal system.   The Executive of a state has an important representative place, as a type of the state's legal unity; it has a weighty function of superintendence, is the fountain of information, the centre and source of advice, the highest organ of administration to the general eye; but it cannot be said to have any place or function of guiding power.   Executive power is diffused by our law throughout the local organs of government; only a certain formal superintendence remains with the authorities at the state capitals.

> Of course this does not apply to the governor's *veto* power, — that contains real energy, — but only to executive functions proper; these are localized, not centralized, after the extremest pattern.

134. Not all of the states have the same central executive officers. All, of course, have governors; twenty-seven have lieutenant governors; all have secretaries of state; all have treasurers; almost all have attorneys-general; and a majority, superintendents of education. Many have also auditors; eleven have comptrollers, and eleven boards of education; three (Massachusetts, New Hampshire, Maine) associate councils with their governors.

> 135. For the rest, there are minor officers of various functions in the different states; superintendents of prisons, for instance, registrars of land offices, superintendents of labor, bureaux of agriculture, commissioners of mines, commissioners of immigration, etc. There is, of course, no uniformity between the administrations of the states as regards these special offices; different states undertake different functions, new or old, and create new, or revive old, offices accordingly.

136. **The governor's term of office** is in almost all of the states either two or four years, although Massachusetts and

Rhode Island give their governors a term of but a single year, while New York and New Jersey elect theirs for three. The lieutenant-governor, where such an officer is elected, has the same term as the governor, and is generally required to have the same qualifications.

137. These *qualifications* consist, almost always, of citizenship of from two to twenty years standing, residence within the state of from one to ten years, and age of from twenty-five to thirty years.

In Maine it is required that the governor shall be a *native-born* citizen. Massachusetts imposes upon candidates for her governor's chair a property qualification, namely, the possession in his own right of freehold property lying within the state, and worth £1000.

138. **The terms of the other principal state officers** are usually the same as the term of the governor, though it is not uncommon to give to treasurers, secretaries of state, attorneys-general, and auditors a longer tenure. The qualifications required of the different officers are of course of the most various nature.

In New York, though the governor and lieutenant-governor hold for three years, the other officers of state are given terms of only two years.

139. The constitutions of many of the states still exhibit the jealousy of long terms of office which was so characteristic of the extreme democratic feeling generated in the colonies by the constant friction between the representatives of the people and officials who owed their offices, not to election, but to royal appointment. The constitution of Mississippi forbids the holding of any office for life or during good behavior; seven states limit official tenure to a maximum period of seven years; Texas makes two years the maximum; and Massachusetts, Virginia, and Maryland give express constitutional sanction to *rotation in office.*

140. Many states effect such a limitation with reference to the tenure of the governor's office by provisions setting bounds to the re-eligibility of the governor. Thus some exclude their governors from successive terms; others allow only a single term to any one man within a specific period of, say, eight years; while still others withhold re-eligibility altogether.

141. Contrast between State and Federal Executives. —
The federal executive was, as we have seen (sec. 38), constituted in quite close accordance with the models of previous
state organization; but the imitation can scarcely be said to
have gone further than the adoption of the suggestion that the
United States should have a single governmental head, a president, because the states had tried and approved a single presidency. For the rest, the president was given the character,
as regards his relations with the other officials of the federal
system, rather of an English sovereign than of a state governor.
Certainly the contrast between the official place and power of
the president and the place and power of the state governors
of the present day is a very sharp and far-reaching contrast
indeed. The president of the United States is the only executive officer of the federal government who is elected; all
other federal officials are appointed by him, and are responsible
to him. Even the chief of them bear to him, in theory at
least, only the relation of advisers; though in fact, it must be
acknowledged, they are in effect his colleagues. Of state officials associated with the governor it may, on the other hand, be
said that both in law and in fact they are colleagues of the governor, in no sense his agents or subordinates, except perhaps
in mere formal precedence. They, like himself, are elected by
the people; he is in no way concerned in their choice. Nor do
they serve him after election. They are not given him as
advisers; they are, on the contrary, co-ordinated with him.
North Carolina, indeed, calls her chief officers of state a 'cabinet'; but they are not dependent upon each other even in
counsel, and they are quite as independent of the governor as
Congress is of the president. The only means of removal to
which the principal officers of the states are subject is, ordi-
narily, *impeachment*, to which the governor also is equally
exposed. Both they and he may be charged with official
crimes and misdemeanors by the house of representatives and
tried, convicted, and removed by the senate of the state. Their

only other responsibility is to the courts of law, to which, like any other citizens, they are answerable, after removal from office, for actual breaches of law. Governor, treasurer, secretary of state, attorney-general, — all state officers alike, serve, not other officers, but the people, who elected them ; upon the people they are dependent, not upon each other ; they constitute no hierarchy, but stand upon a perfect equality.

142. In Delaware, Kentucky, Maryland, New Jersey, Pennsylvania, West Virginia, and Texas, the secretaries of state are appointed by the governor, subject to confirmation by the senate; in several states the attorney-general also is appointed; nor is it uncommon for the state superintendent of education to be an appointee of the governor: and these facts offer apparent contradiction to the statement that the several constituent parts of the state executives stand always apart in complete independence and co-ordination, — especially when it is added that in one or two states officers so important as the secretary of state and the attorney-general *hold during the pleasure of the governor.* But these cases constitute in fact no real exceptions : for the duties of such officers, after their appointment, are prescribed by constitutional provision or by statute, not by the governor; and the governor may remove them, not at his whim, but for just legal cause only. In brief, though appointed by him, they do not depend upon him.

143. **Real Character of a State 'Executive.'** — The governor therefore, is not the 'Executive '; he is but a single piece of the executive. There are other pieces co-ordinated with him over which he has no direct official control, and which are of less dignity than he, only because they have no power to control legislation, as he may do by the exercise of his veto, and because his position is more representative, perhaps, of the state government as a whole, of the people of the state as a unit. Indeed it may be doubted whether the governor and other principal officers of a state government can even when taken together be correctly described as ' the executive,' since the actual execution of the laws does not rest with them but with the local officers chosen by the towns and counties and bound to the central authorities of the state by no real bonds

of responsibility whatever.   Throughout all the states there is a significant distinction, a real separation, between 'state' and 'local' officials; local officials are not regarded, that is, as state officers, but as officers of their districts only, responsible to constituents, not to central authorities.   In all the states, probably without exception, the sheriffs and other county officers, the county treasurers, clerks, surveyors, commissioners, etc., and the town and city officials also, as well as the judges of the courts and the solicitors or district attorneys who represent the public authority before the courts, are chosen by the voters of limited areas, and are regarded, for the most part, as serving, not the state, but *their part of the state*.   Minor 'state' officers there are, — minor officers, that is, who serve ministerially the central offices, — and these are often appointed by the governor; but it is exceptional for the governor to control in any real sense the officials, the local authorities, by whom the laws are in fact put into actual operation.   The president of the United States is the veritable chief and master of the official forces of the federal government; he appoints and in most cases can remove, for cause, all federal marshals, district attorneys, revenue officers, post-office officials.   But the governor of a state occupies no such position; nor does any high 'state' official; the central offices of a state constitute a system of supervision and report often, but seldom a system of control.

144. In Michigan, it is true, all officials not legislative or judicial may be removed by the governor for just legal cause; in New York, too, sheriffs, coroners, district attorneys, and county clerks are removable by the same authority, and in Wisconsin sheriffs, coroners, district attorneys, and registrars of deeds; but such provisions are exceptional, and are not accompanied by any real integration of local government by a system of continuous central control. Government remains disjointed, — still lies in separated parts.

145. **Relations of the Local to the Central Organs of Government in the States.** — It is characteristic of our state organization, therefore, that the counties, townships, and cities into which the states are divided for purposes of local government do not serve as organs of the

states exactly, but rather as independent organisms, constituted what they are by state law, indeed, but after being set up, left to themselves almost as entirely as if they were self-constituted. They elect their own officers and go their own paces in enforcing the general laws of the state.

146. We have not, therefore, local '*self-government*,' in the sense in which Professor Gneist has found that term to be properly used when employed in the light of its Teutonic history; we have, instead, separate local self-direction which is not the application of government, but the play of independent action. Our local areas are not *governed*, in brief; they act for themselves. Self-government implies, when used in its strict historical meaning, that the officers of local administration are officers of the *state*, of the central authority, whatever may be the machinery of their appointment, and that their responsibility is central, not to their neighbors merely. The only sense in which the local units of our state organization are *governed* at all is this, that they act under general laws which are made, not by themselves, but by the central legislatures of the states. These laws are not executed by the central executive authorities, or under their control, but only by local authorities acting in semi-independence. They are, so to say, left to run themselves.

147. **The Governor.** — The usual duties of a state governor may be conveniently summed up under four general heads: (1), as towards the legislature, it is his duty to transmit to the houses at each regular session, and at such other times as may be required, full information concerning the state of the commonwealth, and to recommend to them such measures as seem to him necessary for the public good. It is also his duty in case of necessity for such a step, or upon the requisition of a sufficient number of legislators, to summon the houses to extra session. (2) He is commander-in-chief of the state militia, and as such is bound to see, not only that foreign invasion is repelled, but also that internal order is preserved. (3) He exercises the clemency of the state towards condemned persons, having the right to grant pardons to persons convicted of crime, to remit fines and penalties, under certain conditions, and to remove political disabilities incurred in consequence of conviction of crime; though he exercises these high prerogatives subject always to a definite responsibility to public opinion and to the laws.

In some states, as notably in Pennsylvania, the power of granting pardons is given to the governor, however, only in form, the sanction being made necessary of a Board of Pardons, whose action is semi-judicial.

(4). In all the states except four (Delaware, Rhode Island, Ohio, North Carolina) the governor's assent is made necessary to the validity of all laws not passed over his dissent by a special legislative vote upon a second consideration made in full view of the governor's reasons for withholding his signature.

148. All bills which the governor signs, or upon which he does not take any action within a certain length of time, become law; those which he will not sign he must return to the legislature with a statement of his objections. Generally he must return bills which he thus rejects to the house in which they originated, though in Kansas he must return them always to the House of Representatives.

149. The vote by which a bill may be passed over the governor's veto varies very widely among the states. In Connecticut a mere majority suffices for its second passage; in other states a three-fifths vote is required, in some a two-thirds vote; sometimes a majority of elected members (instead of a special number within a mere quorum) must concur in a second passage; and sometimes two-thirds of the elected members. In Missouri it is provided that the votes of two-thirds of the elected members shall be necessary in the house in which the measure originated, while a mere majority of the other house will suffice.

150. In thirteen of the states the governor is given the power to veto particular items in appropriation bills; as regards all other bills his approval or disapproval must cover all of the measure or none of it.

151. The Secretary of State. — The title 'Secretary of State' borne by a conspicuous officer in each of the states is very apt to mislead those who have studied first the English executive or the functions of our own minister of foreign affairs. The federal Secretary of State is first of all an executive minister, only secondarily a secretary; and the five principal Secretaries of State in England are equally without prominent secretarial functions. They are one and all executive heads of department.

152. The federal Secretary of State is entitled to his official name chiefly by virtue of certain minor duties seldom thought of by the public in connection with the Department of State. He has charge of the

seal of the United States; he preserves the originals of all laws and of
all orders, resolutions, or votes of the houses which have received the
force of law; he furnishes to Congress, besides consular and diplomatic
reports, lists of passengers arrived in the United States from foreign
countries, etc.

153. The chief clerical features of the office which the five Principal
Secretaries of State in England theoretically share (sec.* 693) would
seem to be represented by the necessity of the countersignature of some
one of them to the validity of the sign-manual.

154. The Secretaries of State in the commonwealths of our
Union, on the contrary, can show substantial cause for holding
their title; the making and keeping of records is the central
duty of their office. It is usually their duty to register the
official acts of the governor, to enroll and publish the Acts of
the Legislature, to draw up all commissions issued to public
officers, to keep all official bonds, to record all state titles to
property, to keep and affix, where authorized, the seal of the
commonwealth, to preserve careful records of the boundaries of
the various civil districts (the counties, townships, etc.) of the
state, and to give to all who legally apply duly attested copies
of the public documents in their keeping. In brief, the Secretary's office is the public record office.

155. Often other duties are assigned to the Secretary of State. In
one state, for instance, he is constituted Internal Improvement Commissioner; in another Surveyor-general. But such additional functions
are not, of course, characteristic of his office.

156. It is to the Secretary of State in each commonwealth that the
votes of the state's electors for President and Vice President are returned; it is he who transmits them to the president of the Senate to
be opened in the joint session of the two houses.

157. Votes in state elections also are generally returnable to the
Secretary of State's office, and the Secretary of State is very commonly
one of the state canvassers of election returns. Such duties manifestly
flow very naturally from the general duties of his office.

158. The Comptroller, or that equivalent officer, the state
Auditor, is public accountant. It is his function to examine
and pass upon all claims presented under existing provisions

of law against the state; to audit the accounts of all officers charged with the collection of the revenue of the state, filing their vouchers, and requiring of them the necessary bonds, and crediting them with all sums for which they present the state Treasurer's receipt; to ensure uniformity in the assessment and collection of the public revenue by preparing and furnishing to the local fiscal officers the proper forms and instructions; to issue warrants for all legal disbursements of money from the treasury of the state, keeping a careful account with the state treasurer; to submit his books and accounts at any time to examination by the legislature: in a word, to regulate the assessment, collection, and disbursement of the public moneys.

159. **The State Treasurer** may be said simply to keep the public moneys subject to the warrants of the Comptroller. Without such warrant he can pay out nothing.

160. These, manifestly, are not offices of control. The Comptroller, for example, can generally proceed against local fiscal officers through the local law-representatives of the state, the local states-attorneys, in the ordinary courts, for the purpose of securing the necessary bonds, when these are not promptly or properly given, or of enforcing the payment of moneys withheld or uncollected; and he may make test of the validity or sufficiency of official bonds by any means within his reach; but he has none but this judicial control, this indirect control, that is, exercised through the courts over officers who refuse bond or who neglect the forms and instructions issued to them regarding the assessment and collection of taxes. The whole machinery of control is local, not central, — through courts and states-attorneys who are themselves elected by the same persons, in town or county, by whom the collecting officers are chosen. The local fiscal officers are not, in other words, officers of the state Treasury, but officers of the towns and counties whom the state employs as its agents.

161. **The State Superintendent of Education** often occupies a somewhat different position. It is his prerogative to prescribe the qualifications of teachers and the methods by which they are to be selected; he exercises a thorough inspection of the schools throughout the state; often he is given power to

secure proper reports of school work through special inspectors appointed to act instead of local superintendents whose reports are irregular or unsatisfactory. School administration is recognized to require a certain degree of centralization of authority, and so to constitute a legitimate exception to the general rules as to the constitution of executive power in the states. Still, even the power of a state Superintendent of Education does not often go very much beyond mere supervision. The powers of district or township school directors remain in most cases very absolute as regards the management of the schools. They are governed by statute, not by the state Superintendent.

162. **Constitutional Diffusion of the Executive Power.** — The constitutions of at least seven of the states make very frank confession of the diffusion of executive authority upon which I have dwelt as characteristic of our state system. Thus the constitution of Alabama provides that the executive power "shall consist of the governor, Secretary of State, state treasurer, state auditor, attorney-general, and superintendent of education, and the sheriff for each county." The constitutions of Arkansas, Colorado, Illinois, Minnesota, Pennsylvania, and Texas, make similar enumerations, with the exception of the sheriffs of the counties. The Florida constitution of 1868 provided that the governor should be "assisted by a cabinet of administrative officers" appointed by himself, subject to the confirmation of the Senate; but clothed these officers with functions which made them in fact not assistants but colleagues.

The constitutions of most of the other states declare the executive power to be vested in the governor, but are hardly through with outlining his functions before they provide for the erection of executive departments among which the greater part of executive power shall be parcelled out; so that the arrangement is, in effect, that of those states which declare the executive office to be 'in commission' by enumerating the officers who are to divide its duties.

163. **Full Legal, but no Hierarchical, Control.** — This, then, is the sum of the whole matter: the control of law is thorough and complete: statutes leave to no officer, either central or local, any considerable play of discretionary power: so far as possible they command every officer in every act of his administration. But no hierarchy stands between any officer and the law. The several functions of executive power

are segregated, — each official, so to say, serves his own statute. So thorough is the control attempted by legislation, — and so potent among us is the legal habit and conscience, the law-abiding sense, — that no official control, no hierarchical organization has been thought necessary.

Local Government.

164. General Characteristics. — The large freedom of action and broad scope of function given to local authorities is the distinguishing characteristic of the American system of government. Law is central, in the sense of being uniform and the command of the central legislature in each state; and its prescriptions are minute; but function and executive power are local. There is a single comprehensive statutory plan, but a host of unassociated deputies to carry it into effect, an infinite variety in the local application of its principles. General laws are given to the localities by state legislation, and these laws are generally characterized by a very great degree of particularity and detail of provision; but no central authority has executive charge of their application : each locality must see to it for itself that they are carried out.

165. Duties of Local Government. — The duties of local government include Police, Sanitation, the Care of the Poor, the Support and Administration of Schools, the Construction and Maintenance of Roads and Bridges, the Licensing of Trades, the Assessment and Collection of Taxes, besides the Administration of Justice in the lower grades, the maintenance of Court Houses and Jails, and every other affair that makes for the peace, comfort, and local good government of the various and differing communities of each commonwealth. In many places libraries are included among the institutions given into the charge of the officers of local government. - Of course local officers look to state law for their authority; but practically state administration represents only the unifying scheme of local government. Local administration is *the* administration of the state.

166. **Local Varieties of Organization.** — Almost without exception the states which have been added to the original thirteen by whom the Union was formed have derived their local institutions, whether by inheritance or by imitation, from the mother-states of the Atlantic seaboard. Wherever New England settlers have predominated the *township* has taken quick rootage and had a strong growth; wherever Southern men have gone the *county* has found favor above other forms of local organization; wherever the people from the two sections have met and mixed, as in the early days they met and mixed in New Jersey and Pennsylvania, the same combination or mixture of institutions that is characteristic of the middle Atlantic states is found in full prominence. But in all cases the new foundations in the west have this common feature: they have all been in a greater or less degree artificially contrived. Towns have not grown up in the northwest for the same reasons that led to their growth in New England, in the days when isolation was necessary, and when isolation of course involved compact and complete self-government (secs. 4–6): they have, on the contrary, been deliberately constructed in imitation of New England models. Neither have Western counties been developed by processes of pioneer agricultural expansion such as made the irregular, and in a sense geographically natural, counties of Virginia (secs. 10–12): they have, on the contrary, been geometrically laid off in the exact squares of the government survey because the settlers wanted to reproduce by statute the institutions which in their old homes have been evolved by slow, unpremeditated colonial growth. The institutions of the admitted states, in a word, were transplanted by enactment, whereas the institutions of the original states were almost unconscious adaptations of old custom. It by no means follows that these newer institutions lack naturalness or vigor: in most cases they lack neither, — a self-reliant race has simply re-adapted institutions common to its political habit; but they do lack the individu-

ality and the native flavor often to be found in the institutions in whose likeness they have been made.

167. The differences of institution, then, which show themselves in the east between local government in New England, local government in the South, and local government in the central belt of Atlantic states extend also into the west. There, too, we find the three types, the township type, the county type, and the compound type which stands between the two; but the compound type is in the west naturally the most common: the westerner has had the sagacity to try to combine the advantages of all the experiments tried in the older states, rejoicing in being fettered by no hindering traditions, and profiting by being restrained by no embarrassing incapacity for politics.

Keeping these facts in mind, it will be possible to consider without confusion, the Township, the County, the School District, the Town, and the City as elements of local government in the United States. The different place and importance given to each of these organs in different sections may be noted as we proceed.

168. The Township: Its Historical Origin. — The township is entitled to be first considered in every description of local government in the United States not only because it is a primary unit of administration, but also by reason of its importance and because of its ancient and distinguished lineage. It is a direct lineal descendant from the primitive communal institutions which Cæsar and Tacitus found existing in the vigor of youth among the peoples living in the ancient seats of our race. The New England town was not an American invention; and the settlers upon the northern coasts did not adopt the town system simply because they were obliged to establish themselves in isolated settlements in a harsh climate and among hostile native tribes. We have seen (secs. 4, 5) that they kept together in close settlements for religious purposes, for mutual defence, and for purposes of trade, and that

their settlements were completely isolated by stretches of wild primeval forest; but their form of government, or at least the talent and disposition for it, they brought with them, an inheritance of untold antiquity. Their political organization was simply a spontaneous reproduction of the ancient Germanic Mark (secs.* 222, 765). In most cases they regarded the land upon which they settled as the property of the community, just as their remote barbarian ancestors had done; like those ancestors, they divided out the land among families and individuals or worked it in common as might be decided by public vote in general assembly, in open 'folk-moot' we may call it. This same 'town-meeting,' as they styled it, voted the common discipline, elected the officers, and made the rules of common government: each group of colonists constituted themselves a state with a sovereign primary assembly. They re-established, too, the old principles of folk-land. Whether they tilled their lands in common or not, they had always a communal domain, part of which was kept as open Common for the general pasturage, and the rest of which was given over in parcels, from time to time, for settlement. They were inventing nothing; they were simply letting their race habits and instincts have natural play. Their methods showed signs at almost every point, of course, of having been filtered through intervening English practices; but they rested upon original Teutonic principles.

169. The exceptions to the principle of folk-land occurred where, as in the Hartford, Windsor, and Wethersfield settlements on the Connecticut, the land was held, not in common by the civil community, but in common by a sort of corporation of joint owners under whose supervision the new colonies were established. These joint owners were quite distinct from communal authorities.[1]

170. Absorption of the Town in Larger Units of Government. — It was towns of this primitive pattern that were drawn together ultimately into the New England colonies of the later

[1] See Andrews, *The River Towns of Connecticut* (Johns Hopkins Studies, Seventh Series).

time by the processes I have already described (sec. 838) ; and
of course in becoming parts of larger organizations they lost
to some extent their independence of movement, as well as in
some slight degree their individuality also. In some cases,
as for instance in the coalescence of 'Connecticut' and New
Haven (sec. 18), the establishment of central state legislative control over the towns took the shape of a mere confirmation to them of their old functions and privileges, and in this
way fully recognized their elder and once sovereign place in
the historical development of the commonwealth; but it in all
cases necessarily resulted in their virtual subordination. It
led also to the creation of new areas of local government.
Towns were grouped, at first for judicial purposes only, into
counties, and the counties came in time to furnish a more convenient basis for certain administrative functions once vested
exclusively in the smaller areas. Great cities, too, presently
grew up to demand more complex, less simply and directly
democratic, methods than those of the towns. But no change
has seriously threatened town organization with destruction:
it is still the most characteristic and most vital element of
local government in New England; and it still has substantially the same officers, substantially the same functions that
it possessed at its foundation in America.

> 171. Of course an influx of foreigners has in many places disturbed
> and even impaired the town system, and the cities, which draw to them-
> selves so rapidly the rural population, but which are too big for the
> primitive methods of town government, are powerful disintegrating
> elements in the midst of the old organization; but the new adaptation
> and development of the township in the west, and the tendency to in-
> troduce it in some parts of the south, seem still to promise it honor and
> length of days.

172. **Town-meeting.** — The sovereign authority, the motive
power, of town government is the Town-meeting, the general
assembly of all the qualified voters of the town, which has
reminded so many admiring observers of the ancient Grecian

and Roman popular assemblies and of the *Landsgemeinde* of Switzerland. The regular session of this assembly is held once a year, usually in the Spring,[1] but extra sessions are held from time to time throughout the year as occasion arises, due notice being given both of the time of meeting and of the exact business to be considered. Town-meeting elects all officers, — its regular annual session being the session for elections, — and decides every affair of local interest.[2] It is presided over by a 'Moderator' and attended by the town officers, who must give full account of their administration, and who must set before the Meeting a detailed statement of the sums of money needed for local government. These sums, if approved, are voted by the Meeting and their collection ordered, on the prescribed basis of assessment. Everything that the officials and committees of the town have done is subject to be criticised, everything that they are to do is subject to be regulated by the Meeting.

173. **The Town Officers.** — The officers of the town are certain 'Selectmen,' from three to nine in number, according to the size and needs of the town, who constitute the general executive authority for all matters not otherwise assigned; a Town Clerk, who is the keeper of the town records and registers; a Treasurer; Assessors, whose duty it is to make valuation of all property for tax assessment; a Collector of the taxes voted by the Meeting or required by the county and state authorities; a School Committee; and a variety of lesser officers of minor function, such as Constables, together with certain committees, such as library trustees, etc. Generally there are also overseers of the poor and surveyors of highways.

174. To this corps of officers all the functions of local government belong. The county authorities cannot enter their

---

[1] In Connecticut in the autumn.

[2] In some of the coast towns (townships), as notably in Connecticut, the regulation of the use of the oyster beds is a very prominent question in town-meeting.

domain, but must confine themselves to the judicial duties proper to them and to such administrative matters as the laying out of inter-town roads, the issuing of certain county licenses, the maintenance of county buildings, etc., for the due oversight of which larger areas than the town seem necessary. County expenses are defrayed by taxes raised by the towns: the county authorities apportion such taxes, but lay none.

In Rhode Island the only county officials are those connected with the administration of justice.

175. The Township of the Northwest. — The town may, therefore, be said to exist in New England in its historical character and simplicity, overshadowed here and there by great cities, and everywhere modified and partially subordinated by the later developments of state and county. In the *Northwest*, whither New England emigrants have gone, it has entered another phase and taken on another character, — a character which may perhaps foreshadow its ultimate organization should the country have at any future time the uniform practices of local government now dimly promised by certain incipient forces of institutional interchange and imitation.

176. In the first place, the Northwestern township is more thoroughly integrated with the county than is the New England township: county and township fit together as pieces of the same organism. In New England the township is older than the county, and the county is a grouping of townships for certain purposes; in the Northwest, on the contrary, the county has in all cases preceded the township, and townships are divisions of the county. The county may be considered as the central unit of local government: townships as differentiations within it.

177. The county preceded the township because the county furnishes, for our people, the natural basis of organization for a scattered agricultural population; the township came afterwards, at the suggestion of the New England settlers, as the

natural organization for a population became more numerous and drawn together into closer association.

178. Its Origin. — As all the best authorities on this subject have pointed out, *school organization* supplied the beginnings of the township system in all the more newly settled portions of the country, and is now producing the seeds of it in the South. The western township has sprung out of the school as the New England township of the earliest days sprang out of the church. The government surveyor, who has everywhere preceded final settlement in the west, has in all cases mapped out the land in regular square plots which, for convenience, he has called 'townships,' and in every township Congress has reserved a square mile of land for the endowment of schools. This endowment had to be administered by the settlers, school organization had to be effected, the name township had already been given to the district so endowed, and there was, therefore, naturally school organization on the basis of the township. From this there eventually issued an equally natural growth of local political institutions.[1]

179. Spread of Township Organization. — The development of the township has progressed almost in direct ratio with the development of local government : in many sections of the country, even where population is dense, county organization is still made to suffice for such districts as have not assumed the structure and privileges of village or city incorporation, but wherever any special effort has been made to perfect local rural organization for administrative purposes, the township has been accepted as the best model of political association.

180. It has received its widest acceptance in such middle states as New York and Pennsylvania, and in the great Northwestern states of Michigan, Wisconsin, Illinois, and Minnesota. Elsewhere, in the Middle West, in Ohio, Indiana, and Kansas, for example ; and in such states of

---

[1] See p. 10 of *Local Government in Illinois*, by Dr. Albert Shaw (Johns Hopkins Studies in Historical and Political Science, First Series).

the far West as California, it is less fully developed, and occupies a much more subordinate place as compared with the County. The County, indeed, may be said to be the prevalent unit of local government in California, as well as in Oregon, Nebraska, and Nevada.

181. Township Organization. — The *organization* of the township outside of New England, of course, varies with its development. Where it is most vigorous there is the town-meeting exercising powers strictly defined and circumscribed by statute and somewhat less extensive than the powers of town-meeting in New England, but still covering a multitude of local interests and representing a very real control. Where it is less developed there is no town-meeting, but instead only the processes of popular election to local office. In all cases the 'selectmen' have disappeared: at least we find no officers bearing their name, and no officers possessing exactly their functions. Where the township is most completely organized we find one or more 'supervisors' standing at the front of township administration, who are clothed with the duties of overseers of the poor, who exercise oftentimes a certain control over the finances of the township, and who are, in general function, the presiding and directing authorities of the administration.

182. In Michigan and Illinois a single supervisor presides over each township; and in the former state each supervisor is also tax assessor, while in the latter he is treasurer. In Wisconsin and Minnesota there are three supervisors in each township; in Ohio three nearly equivalent officers called 'trustees.'

183. Where there are several supervisors or trustees in the township, it is common to associate them together as a Board, and under such an arrangement they very closely resemble the New England board of selectmen in their administrative functions. Township boards also exist under the laws of some states in which there is but a single supervisor for each township, being composed, usually, besides the supervisor, of such officers as the town clerk and the Justices of the Peace.

In Michigan such a board has rather extensive supervisory powers;
in Illinois it is a committee of audit simply.

184. The number of township officers of course varies with
the degree of development to which the township system has
attained. In Ohio, where the system is still more or less in
germ, there are, besides the three trustees, no township officers
save a clerk and a treasurer. In Michigan, even, where the
township system is fully accepted, there is neither an assessor
nor a collector of taxes, the supervisor acting as assessor and
the treasurer as collector. In Illinois, on the other hand, there
is always a very full corps of officers: supervisor, collector, assessor, clerk, commissioners of highways, school trustees, justices of the peace, constables, etc.

185. The term of all officers except justices of the peace, road and
school commissioners, and constables, is generally but a single year, as
in New England; the terms of the other officers named are often three
or four years.

186. Where there is a town-meeting the officers are elected by it;
where there is no town-meeting they are of course chosen by ballot.

187. The Township in the Middle Atlantic States. — Of
course it is reversing the historical order to speak of the townships of the middle Atlantic states after discussing the townships of the newer west; but it is not reversing the order of
convenient exposition. The processes of formation are plainly
visible in the west; in the east they are more complex and
obscure, being the formations of history rather than of legislation.

188. The New York township is like the townships of
Michigan and Illinois in its structure and functions; but like
because it is an original, not because it is a copy. Over it
presides a single supervisor who is the treasurer and general
financial officer of the area. It has its clerk, its assessor, its
collector, its commissioners of highways, its constables, its justices of the peace. It has also special overseers of the poor.
An annual town-meeting, under the presidency of the justices

of the peace, or of the town clerk, elects all officers, passes
sundry by-laws, votes taxes for schools and poor-relief, and
constitutes the general governing authority.

In counties containing 300,000 or more inhabitants there is a provision for the election of township officers by ballot.

189. The Pennsylvania Township. — The New York town-
ship system suggested the system of the states about the lakes,
and stands nearest in the order of development to the township of New England. The township of Pennsylvania, on the
other hand, suggests the township system of the next lower belt
of western states. In it there is no town-meeting, but only an
executive machinery. A board of two or three supervisors holding for a term of three years presides over the township, and
has as its most prominent function the care of highways. For
the rest, there are the usual officers, with the somewhat uncommon addition of three auditors. Where the township is charged
with the care of the poor, two special overseers are elected.

190. Origins of Local Government in the Middle States. —
Local government in New York, Pennsylvania, Delaware, and most of
New Jersey runs back, as to a common source, to the system established
in colonial times by the Duke of York as proprietor. Under that system the township was the principal organ of local government. Its
officers were certain constables and overseers; and above the township
was only an artificial ‘ Riding’ presided over by a sheriff. Certain
General Courts levied highway and poor rates, appointed overseers of
highways, etc. After the period of the Duke’s proprietorship, the development of local government in the several parts of his domain
exhibited a considerable variety. The township retained its importance
in New York, but further south, particularly in Pennsylvania, the
county gained the superior place.

191. The Township in the South. — Wherever, in the
south, the principle of local taxation for local schools has been
fully recognized, there the township has begun to show itself,
at least in bud. Virginia, the oldest of the southern states,
and in most respects the type of all the rest in institutional

development, has, since 1870, had the township system in full flower.

192. **In the Virginia townships,** as in those of the middle west, there is no town-meeting, — all officers, down even to the constable, are elected at the polls. Each township has its single supervisor, but, as in Michigan, the supervisor has authority only as a member of a township board, on which the commissioner of roads and the assessor are associated with him. This board is the auditing and general financial authority of the township, has charge of highways, has the usual care of the township property, and the usual general oversight. The clerk of the township is *ex officio* treasurer, and must countersign the warrants of the board. There are special overseers of the poor, but county poor-houses receive paupers sent from the townships. For the rest, there is the usual collector, justice of the peace, and constable. As in New York, the supervisors of the townships collectively constitute the governing board of the county.

North Carolina, also, and West Virginia have adopted to some extent the township system.

The division of power between township and county can be most intelligibly discussed in connection with the following outline of county organization.

193. **The County.** — The natural history of the county is best studied in the south, where, despite the partial, and in Virginia the complete formal, adoption of township organization, the county remains the chief, and almost the only organ of local order and government. We have seen (secs. 10, 11) how natural a basis of government it was for a wide-spread agricultural population. The county was imported into the west by southern settlers, but also found there at first its natural reason for existence in a similarly diffused population. New England immigration and new conditions of industrial and social combination have created the township within the county in the west, as they promise to create it in the south, also (see sec. 191).

194. In all cases it would seem the county was originated for judicial purposes, as an area in and for which courts were to be held, though in such confederate colonies as Connecticut

it was also in part the outgrowth of the union of different groups of once independent towns. In the south the county became also the single area for the administrative organization of local government, being given the functions elsewhere divided between the county and lesser areas like the township. In New England certain general functions of a limited character have been conferred upon it by subtraction from the townships. In the northwest, county and township have been created almost simultaneously and side by side, and are carefully integrated.

195. The American county was of course in the first instance a frontier copy of the English shire; but, of course, the American county affords no analogy in its growth to the growth of its English prototype. The English shire in a great many instances traces its history back to the time when it was a separate Saxon kingdom, and may be said to have as natural boundaries as France; American counties, on the other hand, have all been deliberately 'laid out,' as judicial and administrative subdivisions, and have no independent historical standing.

196. **The southern county,** which undertakes all of local administration, has, of course, a complete set of officers. At its head is a small board of *county commissioners*. Acting under the general superintendence of the commissioners there are generally a county treasurer, auditor, superintendent of roads, superintendent of education, and superintendent of the poor. On its judicial side, the county has its sheriff, its clerk, its ordinary or surrogate, its coroner, and its states-attorney, the latter generally acting for a judicial district inclusive of several counties. The functions of the county, of course, embrace the oversight of education, the maintenance of jails and poor-houses, the construction and repair of highways, and all local matters. County officers are in almost all instances elected by popular vote. Under the southern county system the sheriff is commonly tax-collector.

197. **Where the township ex**ists there is great variety of county organization, almost the only point of common likeness

being the organization of justice. The county always has its sheriff, and generally its separate courts with the usual coroner and clerk. The variety exists in the domain of administrative structure. Sometimes, as in New York, Michigan, and Illinois, the county administrative authority is a board composed of the supervisors of all the townships; sometimes, as in Pennsylvania and Minnesota, the county authority is a board of three commissioners. In Wisconsin the county board consists of members each of whom is chosen by two or more townships. Where the county is given least power,. as in New England, its administrative functions hardly extend beyond the maintenance of such county buildings as the jail and court-house, the granting of certain licenses, and the partial supervision of the highway system. In New York and the northwest the county authorities often undertake the relief of the poor, sometimes exercise an extensive control over the debt-contracting privileges of the smaller areas, often audit the accounts of local officers, and supervise taxation for purposes of equalization.

Where townships exist, then, the division of functions may be said to be as follows : the township is the area for the administration of schools, for the relief of the poor (unless by popular vote this function is given to the county), police, construction and maintenance of highways, sanitation; the county is the area for the administration of justice, for the maintenance of jails, courthouses, and sometimes poorhouses, for tax equalization, and often for the exercise of certain other general supervisory powers.

198. Villages, Boroughs, Cities. — Counties and townships are areas of rural organization only; with the compacting of population in great towns and cities other and more elaborate means of organization become necessary, and a great body of constitutional and statutory law has grown up in the states concerning the incorporation of such urban areas. There is no municipal corporations act in any of our states such as that under which, in England, cities of all sizes may acquire the

privileges and adopt the organization of full borough government (sec.* 794): the largest towns are left, under our system,
to depend for their incorporation upon special acts of legislation. The great cities of the country consequently exhibit a
great variety of political structure, and even cities in the same
state often differ widely in many material points of organization and function.

199. The electors or freeholders of less populous districts
are, however, in most of the states empowered to obtain a simple sort of urban organization and considerable urban powers,
by certain routine processes, from the courts of law; *villages*
(as they are called in New York), *boroughs* (as they are styled
in Pennsylvania), *towns* (as they are sometimes designated in
the south), [1] *cities of the lesser grades* (in states where they are
classified according to population), may usually get from the
courts as of course, upon proof of the necessary population
and of the consent of freeholders or electors, the privilege of
erecting themselves into municipal corporations under general
acts passed for the purpose; just as private joint-stock companies may get leave to incorporate upon showing to the court
evidence of the possession of the necessary membership, stock,
or paid-up capital.

200. The town or borough is of course, however, a public, not a
private, corporation, receiving by delegation certain powers of government; and many states have left with their legislatures the power to
create all public corporations by special act. The incorporation of
towns is not, therefore, universally governed by general statute.

201. **The Authorities of urban districts** thus erected into
separate corporations succeed, generally, to all the powers
of township officers within their area and constitute a local
body apart, though no town or city ever altogether ceases to
be a part of the county in which it lies. It continues to pay

[1] The name town when used in New England always means, not an
urban district, but a township.

county taxes and its electors continue to take their part in the choice of county officials. The special organization which these statutory towns receive is unlike that of either county or township principally in this, that they have at the front of their government a representative, quasi-legislative, body, an elected council, that is, which within its sphere is a law-making authority.

202. **A common model of organization** is : a mayor, president, or chief burgess ; a small council of trustees, given extensive power of making by-laws, considerable power of taxation for local improvements as well as for local administration, and other powers of local direction which quite sharply differentiate it from the merely executive boards often found in the townships and always found in the counties ; a treasurer ; a clerk ; a collector ; a street commissioner ; sometimes overseers of the poor ; and generally such other minor officers as the council see fit to appoint.

203. **Organization of Government in Cities.** — The difference between the organization of these smaller urban areas and the organization of great cities is a difference of complexity not only but often also a difference of kind. Cities, we have seen (sec. 122), are often given a separate judicial organization, being made in effect separate judicial circuits or counties, with their own courts, sheriffs, coroners, and state-attorneys. They are given also, of course, larger councils, with larger powers ; a larger corps of officers ; and greater independence than other local areas possess.

204. **The council** of a great city usually consists of two sections or ' houses,' — a board of *aldermen* and a board of *common councilmen*, differing very much as the two houses of a state legislature differ, in the number and size of the districts which their members represent. In the cities of New York State, however, there is but a single legislative chamber, called sometimes the Board of Aldermen, sometimes the Common Council.

205. These boards always constitute the law-making (or rather *ordinance*-making) and taxing power of the city ; and always until recent years they have been constituted overseers of administration also, by being given the power to control it not only by withholding moneys,

but also through direct participation in the power of appointment to the
minor city offices, — all those, that is to say, not filled by popular election. The chief officers of every city have usually been elected, but
all others have, as a rule, been appointed by the mayor subject to confirmation by the city council. The tendency of all very recent legislation with reference to the constitution of city governments has been to
concentrate executive power, and consequently executive responsibility,
in the hands of the mayor, leaving to the council only its ordinance-
making power and its function of financial control. Some of the most
recent charters have even extended the appointing power of the mayor
so as to include the most important executive offices of the city administration. It has been found impossible to prevent corrupt influences
determining the action of councils upon appointments. A numerous
body will, just because it is numerous, be practically irresponsible, and
where there is irresponsibility, the temptation to immorality suffers
little check.

206. **School Administration.** — Wherever the public school
exists there we find the School District the administrative
area for educational purposes. Where the county system prevails the county is divided into school districts; where the
township system prevails the township is divided into school
districts. In every case there are district directors or trustees
who control school administration, and control it so absolutely
as to prevent in great part the existence of any uniform
system of education for the whole state; but where the township system prevails there is generally more participation on
the part of the people, gathered in district-meeting, in school
administration, and generally a fuller power of local taxation.

207. In New England recent years have been witnessing the disap-
pearance of the school district in some states, and its absorption by
the township. Thus in Maine and in Connecticut school administration
is in many places being transferred from district to township officers,
and the township is thereby being made the school area. This absorption is left, however, to local option.

208 **In the Northwest** schools usually receive support
from three distinct sources: from the land granted to each
school district by the federal government; from a general state

tax for education, whose proceeds are distributed among the townships, to be further distributed by the township authorities among the districts; and from district taxes levied by the district directors.   In New England there is generally state and township taxation for the support of the schools. In the south, under the county system, there is state taxation only, for the most part, save in certain exceptional localities, and in the greater towns.

209. Nowhere is there sufficient centralization of control. State superintendents or other central educational authorities are without real administrative powers; county superinten- dents seldom have much authority; township trustees or committees, as a rule, have little more than a general super- vision and power of advice; usually the directors of the smallest area have the greater part of the total of administra- tive authority, applying their *quota* of even the state taxes according to their own discretion.   The result is, variety in the qualifications of teachers, variety in the method of their choice, variety in courses of study, variety in general efficiency.

210. **Taxa**tion. — The most striking feature regarding local taxation in the United States is, the strict limitations put upon it by statute.   Commonly no local authorities can tax beyond a certain fixed percentage of the appraised value of the property of their district.   Under the county system, requisition is made upon the officers of the counties for the taxes voted by the legislature for state purposes, and the county boards raise them, together with the county taxes, upon the basis of the county assessment.   Where the township exists, the process goes one step further: requisition is made upon the townships for both the state and county taxes, and the townships raise these, together with their own taxes, upon the basis of the assessment made by their own assessors.

211. An effort is made in most of the states, however, to equalize assessments.   Some county authority acts as *a board of equalization* with reference to the assessments returned by

the assessors of the several townships, and above the equalization boards of the counties there is generally a state board of equalization, whose duty it is to harmonize and equalize, upon appeal, taxation in the several counties. Appeals always lie from the local assessors to these boards of equalization. The system is, however, only partially successful. It has proved practically impossible, under the present system of localized authority, to avoid great varieties and inequalities of assessment: local officials try to cut down the shares of their districts in the general taxes as much as possible.

212. **General Remarks on Local Government.** — Several features observable in our systems of local government taken as a whole are worthy of remark. (1) In the first place, outside of the towns and cities, the separately incorporated urban districts, there is a marked absence of representative, law-making bodies. Universally local officers and boards have merely executive powers and move within narrow limits set by elaborate statute law.

(2) In the second place, where there are local law-making bodies, they act under strict constitutional law: under charters, that is, possessing thus a strong resemblance, of *kind*, to state legislatures themselves.

(3) In the third place, central control of local authorities exists only in the enforcement, in the regular law courts, of charters and general laws: there is nowhere any central Local Government Board with discretionary powers of restriction or permission.

(4) In the fourth place, relatively to the central organs of the state, local government is the most vital part of our system: as compared either with the federal government or with local authorities, the central governments of the states lack vitality not only, but do not seem to be holding their own in point of importance. They count for much in legislation, but, so far, for very little in administration.

THE FEDERAL GOVERNMENT.

213. **The Constitution of the United States** does not contain all the rules upon which the organization of the federal government rests. It says that there shall be a Congress which shall exercise the law-making power granted to the general

government; a President who shall be charged with the execution of the laws passed by Congress; and a Supreme Court which shall be the highest court of the land for the determination of what is lawful to be done, either by individuals, by the state governments, or by the federal authorities, under the Constitution and laws. It prescribes also in part the organization of Congress. But it does not command how Congress shall do its work of legislation, how the President shall be enabled to perform his great function, or by what machinery of officers and subordinate courts the Supreme Court shall be assisted in the exercise of its powers. It leaves all detail of operation to be arranged by statute : and statute accordingly plays a very important part in the organization of the government.

> The Constitution thus furnishes only the great foundations of the system. Those foundations rest upon the same firm ground of popular assent that supports the several constitutions of the states. Framed by a federal convention and adopted by representative conventions in the states, it stands altogether apart from ordinary law both in character and sanction.

214. **Amendment of the Constitution.** — The Constitution cannot be amended without the consent of two-thirds of Congress and three-fourths of the states. Amendments may be *proposed* in one of two ways : either (*a*) two-thirds of the members of each house of Congress may agree that certain amendments are necessary; or (*b*) the legislatures of two-thirds of the states may petition Congress to have a general convention called for the consideration of amendments, and such a convention, being called, may propose changes. In both cases the mode of *adoption* is the same. Every change proposed must be submitted to the states, to be voted upon either by their legislatures or by state conventions called for the purpose, as Congress may determine. Any amendment which is agreed to by three-fourths ·of the states becomes a part of the Constitution.

The fifteen amendments so far made to the Constitution were all proposed by Congress. No general constitutional convention has been called since the adjournment of the great body by which the Constitution was framed in 1787.

215. None of the written constitutions of Europe are so difficult of alteration as our own. In Germany, as we have seen (sec.* 404), a provision changing the imperial constitution passes just as an ordinary law would pass, the only limitation upon its passage being that fourteen negative votes in the *Bundesrath* will defeat it (14 out of 58). In France (sec.* 318) constitutional amendments pass as ordinary laws do, except that they must be adopted by the two houses of the legislature acting, not separately in Paris, but jointly at Versailles, as a National Assembly. In Switzerland such amendments must pass both houses of the federal legislature and must also be approved, in a popular vote, by a majority of the voters, *and* by a majority of the Cantons (sec.* 556). In England the distinction between constitutional law and statute law can hardly be said to exist (see sec.* 730).

See, also, for a further exposition of constitutional differences between modern states, Chap. XII.*

216. **The Federal Territory.** — The territory of the United States is of two different sorts: there is (*a*) the District of Columbia, which the nation owns as the seat of its government, and the arsenals and dock-yards, which it has acquired from the states for military purposes; and (*b*) the great national property, the territories, which the federal authorities hold in trust for the nation as a seed-bed for the development of new states.

217. **The District of Columbia.** — It would have been inconvenient for the federal government to have no territory of its own on which to build its public offices and legislative halls, and where it could be independent of local or other state regulations. The Constitution itself therefore provided that Congress should have exclusive authority within any district not more than ten miles square which any state might give the federal government for its own uses. Acting upon this hint, Maryland and Virginia promptly granted the necessary territory, it having been decided to establish the seat of govern-

ment upon the Potomac.   The home-land of the federal government, thus acquired, was laid out under the name of the
District of Columbia : there the public buildings were erected,
and there, after the removal of the government offices thither
in 1800, the city of Washington grew up.

218. The first Congress of the United States met in New York
City; there the first President was inaugurated, and the organization
of the new government effected.   In 1790 it was determined that the
federal officers should live and Congress meet in Philadelphia (as the
Continental Congresses and the congress of the Confederation had
done) for ten years; after that, in the district specially set apart for
the use of the federal government.

219. The creation of this federal home-plot is a feature peculiar to
our own federal arrangements.   Berlin, of course, is the capital of
Prussia, not the exclusive seat, or in any sense the property, of the
imperial government.   Berne, too, is cantonal, not federal, ground.   Our
government would have been in the same case as those of Germany
and Switzerland had our federal authorities remained the guests of
New York or Pennsylvania.

220. The several *arsenals and dock-yards* established by the federal
government in different parts of the Union are built upon land granted
to the federal government by the states in which they lie for such special
use, and remain the property of that government only so long as used
for the purposes contemplated in the grants.

221. **The Territories.** — As the different parts of our vast
national domain have been settled it has been divided, under
the direction of Congress, into portions of various sizes, generally about the area of the larger states, though sometimes
larger than any state save Texas.   These portions have been
called, for want of a better name, *Territories,* and have been
given governments constituted by federal statute.   First they
have been given governors and judges appointed by the President; then, as their population has become numerous and sufficiently settled in its ways of living, they have been given legislatures chosen by their own people and clothed with the
power to make laws subject to the approval of Congress; finally,
upon becoming still more developed, they have been granted as

full law-making powers as the states.   The territorial stage of their development passed, the most important of them have one by one been brought into the Union as states.

Until 1803 the only territory of the United States consisted of the lands this side the Mississippi which had belonged to the thirteen original states individually, and had by them been granted to the general government. In 1803 the vast tract known as 'Louisiana' was bought; in 1848, by conquest, and in 1852, by negotiation, the Pacific coast lands were acquired from Mexico; in 1842 Oregon was purchased from England.

222. **The post-offices, federal court chambers, custom houses,** and other like buildings erected and owned by the general government in various parts of the country are held by the government upon the ordinary principles of ownership, just as they might be held by a private corporation. Their sites are not separate federal territory.

223. **Congress.** — As in the states, so in the federal government, the law-making power is vested in a double legislature, a Congress consisting of a Senate and a House of Representatives.   Unlike the two houses of a state legislature, however, the two houses of Congress have distinct characters: the Senate differs from the House not only in the number of its members, but also in the principle of its composition.   It represents the federal principle upon which the government rests, for its members represent the states.   The House of Representatives, on the other hand, represents the national principle upon which also the government has now been finally established, without threat of change: its members represent the people.

224. **The Senate.** — The Senate consists of two representatives from each of the states of the Union.   It has, therefore, the states being forty-two in number, eighty-four members.[1]   Each senator is elected, for a term of six years, by the legislature of the state which he represents; and a state legislature is free to choose any one as senator who has been a citizen of

---

[1] Since the admission of Washington, Montana, North Dakota, and South Dakota, which became states July 1, 1889.

the United States nine years, who has reached the age of thirty, and who is at the time of the election a resident of the state which he is chosen to represent.

225. The Constitution directed that, immediately after coming together for its first session, the Senate should divide its members, by lot, as nearly as it could into three equal groups; that the members of one of these groups should vacate their seats after the expiration of two years, the members of another after the expiration of four years, and the members of the third after the expiration of six years; after which arrangement had been accomplished, the term of every senator was to be six years as provided. It was thus brought about that one-third of the membership of the Senate is renewed by election every two years. The result is, that the Senate has a sort of continuous life, — no one election year affects the seats of more than one-third of its members.

226. The Senate is, as I have said, the *federal* house of Congress, its members represent the states as the constituent members of the Union. They are not, however, in any sense delegates of the governments of the states. They are not subject to be instructed as to their votes, as members of the German *Bundesrath* are, by any state authority (sec.* 405), not even by the legislatures which elected them; each senator is entitled and expected to vote according to his own individual opinion. Senators, therefore, may be said to represent, not the governments of the states, but the people of the states organized as corporate bodies politic.

227. There is no rule which obliges senators from the same state to vote together, after the fashion once imperative in the Congress of our own Confederation (sec. 35), and still imperative in the German *Bundesrath* (sec.* 406), — each senator represents his state, not in partnership, but singly.

228. The *equal* representation of the states in the Senate, of course, more strictly conforms to the federal principle than does the unequal representation characteristic of the German *Bundesrath* (sec.* 406); but the rule observed in Germany, that the representatives of each state must vote together, must, in turn, be allowed to be more strictly consistent with the idea of state representation than is the rule of individual voting followed in our Senate.

229. **The Vice-President of the United States** is president of the Senate.   Unless the President die, this is the only function of the Vice-President.   He is not a member of the Senate, however; he simply presides over its sessions.   He has a vote only when the votes of the senators are equally divided upon some question and his vote becomes necessary, therefore, for a decision.   If the President die, he becomes President.

230. **Organization of the Senate.** — The Senate makes its own rules of procedure, the Vice-President being of course bound to administer whatever rules it adopts.   Naturally the internal organization of the body is the matter with which its rules principally concern themselves, and the most important feature of that organization is the division of the members of the Senate into standing committees; into small groups, that is, to each of which is entrusted the preparation of a certain part of the Senate's business.   The Senate itself would not, of course, have time to look into the history and particulars, the merits and bearings, of every matter brought before it; these committees are, therefore, constituted to act in its stead in the preliminary examination and shaping of the measures to be voted on.   Whenever any proposal is made concerning any important question, that proposal is referred to the standing committee which has been commissioned to consider questions of the particular class to which the proposed action belongs. The committee takes the proposal and considers it, in connection with all other pending proposals relating to the same subject, and reports to the Senate what it thinks ought to be done with reference to it, — whether it is advisable to take any action or not, and if it is advisable to act, what action had best be taken.

> Thus there is a Committee on Finance, to which all questions affecting the revenue are referred; a Committee on Appropriations, which advises the Senate concerning all votes for the spending of moneys; a Committee on Railroads, which considers all railroad questions; a Committee on Foreign Affairs, which prepares for consideration all questions touching our relations with foreign governments, etc., etc.

231. Influence of the Standing Committees. — Its standing committees have, of course, a very great influence upon the action of the Senate. The Senate is naturally always inclined to listen to their advice, for each committee necessarily knows much more about the subjects assigned to it for consideration than the rest of the senators can know. Its committee organization may be said to be of the essence of the legislative action of the Senate : for of course the leadership to which a legislative body consigns itself is of the essence of its method and must affect, not the outward form merely, but the whole character also of its action. Under every great system of government except our own, leadership in legislation belongs for the most part to the ministers, to the Executive, which stands nearest to the business of governing; it is a central, and, as evidenced by its results, extremely important characteristic of our system that our legislatures *lead themselves,* or, rather, that they are led along the several lines of legislation by separate and disconnected groups of their members.

232. The Senate and the Executive. — One of the chief uses of the committees is to obtain information for the Senate concerning the affairs of the government. But, inasmuch as the executive branch of the government is quite separate from Congress, it is often very difficult for the Senate to find out through its committees all that it wishes to know about the condition of affairs in the executive departments. The action of the two houses upon some questions must of course be greatly influenced, and should be greatly influenced, by what they can learn of administrative experience in the departments in such matters, and the Senate, as well as the House also, has the right to ask what questions it pleases of executive officers, either through its committees or by requiring a written report to be made directly to itself by some head of department. Upon financial questions, for example, the Senate or its Finance Committee must constantly wish to know the experience of the Treasury. But it is not always easy to get legislative questions fully and correctly answered : for the officers of the government are in no way responsible to either house for their official conduct : they belong to an entirely separate and independent branch of the government : only such high crimes and misdemeanors as lay them open to impeachment expose them to the power of the houses. The committees are, therefore, frequently prevented from doing their work of inquiry well, and the Senate has to act in the dark. Under other systems of government, as we have seen (secs.* 327, 328, 422 et seq., 464, 533, 686-9, etc.), the ministers are always present in the legislative bodies to be questioned and dealt with directly, face to face.

233. **The President Pro Tempore.** — It is the practice of the Senate to make itself independent of all chances of the Vice-President's absence by electing statedly from its own membership a president *pro tempore*, to act in case of the absence or disability of the Vice-President.

234. **The House of Representatives.** — The House of Representatives represents, not the states, but the people of the United States. It represents them, however, not in the mass, but by states; representation is apportioned among the states severally according to population, and no electoral district crosses any state boundary.

235. **Apportionment of Representatives.** — Congress itself decides by law how many representatives there shall be; it then divides the number decided upon among the states according to population; after which each state is divided by its own legislature into as many districts as it is to have representatives, and the people of each of these districts are entitled to elect one member to the House. The only limitation put by the Constitution itself upon the number of representatives is, that there shall never be more than one for every thirty thousand inhabitants. The first House of Representatives had, by direction of the Constitution itself, sixty-five members, upon the proportion of one to every thirty-three thousand inhabitants. The number has, of course, grown, and the proportion decreased, with the growth of population. A census is taken every ten years, and the rule is to effect readjustments and a redistribution of representation after every census.

At present there are three hundred and thirty members in the House, and the states are given one member for every 154,325 of their inhabitants. In cases where a state has many thousands more than an even number of times that many inhabitants, it is given an additional member to represent the balance. Thus, if it have four times 154,325 inhabitants, and a very large fraction over, it is given five members instead of four only. If any state have less than 154,325, it is given one member, notwithstanding, being entitled to at least one by constitutional provision.

There are at present seven states which have but one representative apiece; namely, Delaware, Colorado, Nevada, Oregon, Washington, Montana, and North Dakota. But these states, like the rest, have two senators each.

The reason for allowing a state an extra representative when there is a large fraction remaining over after a division of its population by the standard number 154,325, is, of course, that the apportionment of representatives is made according to states, and not by an even allotment among the people of the country taken as a whole, and that under such a system a perfectly equal division of representation is practically impossible. Congress makes the most equitable arrangement that is practicable each time that it re-apportions the membership of the House upon the basis of the decennial census which Congress directs to be taken for this purpose in pursuance of a special constitutional command.

236. Elections to the House. — Any one may be chosen a representative who has reached the age of twenty-five years, has been a citizen of the United States for seven years, and is at the time of his election an inhabitant of the state from one of whose districts he is chosen. The term of a representative is two years: and two years is also the term of the whole House; for its members are not chosen a section at a time, as the senators are; the whole membership of the House is renewed every second year. Each biennial election creates 'a new House.'

237. Although the Senate has a continuous life, we speak habitually of different ' Congresses,' as if a new *Congress*, instead of a new House of Representatives merely, were chosen biennially. Thus the Congress of 1887–'89 was known as the fiftieth Congress, because the House of Representatives of that period was the fiftieth that had been elected since the government was established.

238. Federal law does not determine who shall vote for members of the House of Representatives. The Constitution

provides, simply, that all those persons in each state who are qualified under the constitution and laws of the state to vote for members of the larger of the two houses of the state legislature may vote also for members of the House of Representatives of the United States. The franchise is regulated, therefore, entirely by state law.

239. **In the fourteenth amendment** to the Constitution (passed 1866-'68) a very great pressure is, by intention at least, brought to bear upon the states to induce them to make their franchise as wide as their adult male population. For that amendment provides that, should any state deny to any of its male citizens who are twenty-one years of age the privilege of voting for members of the more numerous branch of its own legislature (and thus, by consequence, the privilege of voting for representatives in Congress), for any reason except that they have committed crime, its representation in Congress shall be curtailed in the same proportion that the number of persons so excluded from the franchise bears to the whole number of male citizens twenty-one years of age in the state. This provision has in practice, however, proved of little value. It is practically impossible for the federal authorities to get at the facts necessary to ascertain any such proportion.

240. **Organization of the House.** — The House, like the Senate, has its own rules, regulative of the number and duties of its officers and of its methods of doing business; and these rules, like those of the Senate, are chiefly concerned with the creation and empowering of a great number of standing committees. The committees of the House are not, however, elected by ballot, as the committees of the Senate are; they are appointed by the presiding officer of the House, the 'Speaker'; and this power of the Speaker's to appoint the committees of the House makes him one of the most powerful officers in the whole government. For the committees of the House are even more influential than those of the Senate in determining what shall be done with reference to matters referred to them: they as a matter of fact have it in their power to control almost all the acts of the House. The Senate, being a comparatively small body, has time to consider fully

the reports of its committees, and generally manages to control its own conclusions.   But the House is too large to do much debating: it must be guided by its committees or it must do nothing.   It is this fact which makes the Speaker's power of appointment so vastly important: he determines who shall be on the committees, and the committees determine what the House shall do.   He nominates those who shape legislation.

241. The appointing power of the Speaker often makes his election a very exciting part of the business of each new House : for he is always selected, of course, with reference to what he will do in constituting the principal committees.

242. The House of Representatives is not given a president by the Constitution, as the Senate is.   It elects its own presiding officer, whose name, of 'Speaker,' is taken from the usage of the English House of Commons, whose president was so called because whenever, in the old days, the Commons went into the presence of the king for the purpose of laying some matter before him, or of answering a summons from him, their president was their spokesman or Speaker.   This name is used also in the legislative bodies of all the English colonies, — wherever, indeed, English legislative practices have been directly inherited.

243. The House has so many standing committees that every representative is a member of one or another of them, — but many of the committees have little or nothing to do: some of them, though still regularly appointed, have no duties assigned them by the rules.   The most important committee is that on Appropriations, which has charge of the general money-spending bills introduced every year to meet the expenses of the government, and which, by virtue of its power under the rules to bring its reports to the consideration of the House at any time, to the thrusting aside of whatever matter, virtually dominates the House by controlling its use of its time.   Special appropriation bills, which propose to provide moneys for the expenses of single departments, — as, for example, the Navy Department or the War Department, — are, by a recent rule of the House, taken out of the hands of the Committee on Appropriations and given to the committees on the special departments concerned.   Scarcely less important than the Committee on Appropriations, though scarcely so busy as it, is the Committee on Ways and Means, which has charge of questions of taxation. It is, of course, to the appointment of such committees that the Speaker pays most attention.   Through them his influence is most potent.

Some members of the House are considered to be entitled, because of their long service and experience in Congress, to be put on important committees, and on every committee there must be representatives of both parties in the House. But these partial limitations upon the Speaker's choice do not often seriously hamper him in exercising his preferences.

244. The House has to depend, just as the Senate does, upon its standing committees for information concerning the affairs of the government and the policy of the executive departments, and is just as often and as much embarrassed because of its entire exclusion from easy, informal, and regular intercourse with the departments. They cannot advise the House unless they are asked for their advice; and the House cannot ask for their advice except indirectly through its committees, or formally by requiring written reports.

245. **Acts of Congress.** — In order to become a law or Act of Congress a bill must pass both houses and receive the signature of the President. Such is the ordinary process of legislation. But the President may withhold his signature, and in that case the measure which he has refused to sanction must receive the votes of two-thirds of the members of each house, given upon a re-consideration, before it can go upon the statute book. The President is given ten days for the consideration of each measure. If he take no action upon it within the ten days, or if within that period he sign it, its provisions become law; if within the ten days he inform Congress by special message that he will not sign the bill, returning it to the house in which it originated with a statement of his reasons for not signing it, another passage of the measure by a majority of two-thirds in each house is required to make it a law.

There are, therefore, three ways in which a bill may become law: either (a) by receiving the approval of a majority in each house, and the signature of the President, appended within ten days after its passage by the houses; or (b) by receiving the approval of a majority in each house, and not being acted upon by the President within ten days after its passage; or (c) by receiving the approval of two-thirds of each house after having been refused signature by the President within ten days after its passage by a majority in each house. If Congress adjourn before the expiration of the ten days allowed the President to consider bills sent him, such bills lapse unless he has signed them before the adjournment.

246. Neither house can do any business (except send for absent members or adjourn) unless a majority of its members are present, — a majority being in the case of all our legislatures, both state and federal, the necessary *quorum*.

247. In the practice of some foreign legislatures the quorum is much less than a majority of the members. In the English House of Commons, for instance, it is only forty members, although the total number of members of the House of Commons is six hundred and seventy.

248. When it is said that under certain circumstances a bill must be passed by a vote of two-thirds in order to become a law, it is understood to mean that it must be voted for by two-thirds of the members *present*, not necessarily by that proportion of the whole membership of the body. In the case of bills which the President refuses to sign, however, the Constitution expressly says that it cannot be made law unless a second time passed by *two-thirds of each House.*

249. A bill may 'originate' in either house, unless it be a bill relating to the raising of revenue. In that case it must originate in the House of Representatives, though the Senate may propose what amendments it pleases to a revenue bill, as to any other which comes to it from the House.

Of course, if one of the houses pass a bill, and the other house amend it, the changes so proposed must be adopted by the house in which the bill originated before it can be sent to the President and be made a law. When the two houses disagree about amendments they appoint conference committees ; that is to say, each house appoints a committee to consult with a similar committee appointed by the other house, to see what can be done towards bringing about an agreement between the two houses upon the points in dispute.

250. **The Federal Judiciary: its Jurisdiction.** — The Judiciary of the United States consists of a Supreme Court, Circuit Courts, and District Courts. Its organization and functions rest more than do those of either of the other branches

of the general government upon statute merely, instead of upon constitutional provision. The Constitution declares that "the judicial power of the United States shall be vested in one supreme court, and in such inferior courts as the Congress may, from time to time, ordain and establish," and that "the judges, both of the supreme and inferior courts, shall hold their offices during good behavior and shall, at stated times, receive for their services a compensation which shall not be diminished during their continuance in office." It provides also that the judicial power of the federal government shall extend to all cases in law or equity which may arise under the Constitution, laws, or treaties of the United States; to all cases affecting ambassadors, other public ministers, and consuls; to all admiralty and maritime cases; to controversies in which the United States is a party, controversies between two or more states, between a state and citizens of another state (the state being the suitor), between citizens of different states, between citizens of the same state claiming lands under grants from different states, and between a state or its citizens and foreign states, citizens, or subjects. And it directs that in cases affecting ambassadors, other public ministers and consuls, and in cases in which a state is a party the supreme court shall have original jurisdiction; while in all other cases it is to have appellate jurisdiction only, "with such exemptions, and under such regulations, as the Congress shall make."

251. The judicial power of the federal government is thus made to embrace two distinct classes of cases : (a) those in which it is manifestly proper that its authority, rather than the authority of a state, should control, *because of the nature of the questions involved :* for instance, admiralty and maritime cases, navigable waters being within the exclusive jurisdiction of the federal authorities, and cases arising out of the Constitution, laws, or treaties of the United States or out of conflicting grants made by different states. (b) Those in which, *because of the nature of the parties to the suit,* the state courts could not properly be allowed jurisdiction, cases affecting, for instance, foreign ambassadors, who are accredited to the government of the United States and with whom our

only relations are national relations, whose privileges rest upon the sovereignty of the states they represent; or cases in which the state courts could not have complete jurisdiction because of the residence of the parties; for instance, suits arising between citizens of different states.

It is always open to the choice of a citizen of one state to sue a citizen of another state in the courts of the latter's own domicile, but the courts of the United States are the special forum provided for such cases.

252. Power of Congress over the Judiciary. — But these provisions of the Constitution leave Congress quite free to distribute the powers thus set forth among the courts for whose organization it is to provide, and even, if it so chooses, to leave some of them entirely in abeyance. In other words, the Constitution defines the sphere of the judicial power of the United States, while Congress determines how much of that sphere shall be occupied, by what courts and in what manner, subject to what rules and limitations.

With regard to the organization of the judiciary Congress determines not only what courts shall be created inferior to the supreme court, but also of what number of judges the supreme court shall consist, what their compensation and procedure shall be, and what their specific duties in the administering of justice. It might also determine, should it see fit, what qualifications should be required of all occupants of the supreme bench.

253. The Existing Federal Courts. — In pursuance of these powers, Congress has passed the Judiciary Act of September, 1789, and the Acts amendatory thereto upon which the national judiciary system now rests. As at present constituted, *the supreme court* consists of a chief justice and eight associate justices. It is required to hold annual sessions in the city of Washington, — sessions which begin on the second Monday of each October, — any six of the justices constituting a quorum. Next below the supreme court are a set of *circuit courts*. These are, in theory, courts held in different parts of the country by the justices of the supreme court sitting separately; but in reality the business of the supreme court is so great in amount and so engrossing in character that the justices can by no means regularly attend the sessions of the circuit courts. The area of the United States (exclusive of the territories) is divided into nine circuits, one justice of the supreme court is assigned, by the appointment of the court itself, to each of these circuits, and in addition special circuit judges are appointed who act quite independently of the justices, often holding court separately, in another part of the circuit, at the same time that the justices are themselves holding circuit court. The circuits are divided into districts, which, like Congressional districts, never cross state lines; and for each of these districts there has been established a district court. Some of the less populous states constitute each a single district; others are divided into two, while still others furnish sufficient business to warrant their being divided into three. The district courts are the lowest courts of the federal series. The circuit courts sit in the several districts of each circuit successively, and the law requires that each justice of the supreme court shall sit in each district of his circuit at least once every two years.

254. **The division of jurisdiction** between the circuit and district courts is effected by act of Congress; and, inasmuch as Congress has not seen fit to vest in the courts complete jurisdiction over *all* cases arising under the Constitution, laws, and treaties of the United States, but has given to each court power in certain specified cases, and left the rest in abeyance, it would be impossible to give in brief compass a detailed account of the jurisdiction of the several courts. It must suffice for present purposes to say, that the district courts are given cognizance of certain civil cases within the grant of the Constitution, subject to appeal to the circuit courts when the sum involved exceeds $ 50; that they have exclusive jurisdiction of admiralty and maritime cases, an appeal lying to the circuit courts; and that as regards crimes punishable by federal law, their jurisdiction is concurrent with that of the circuit courts, except in case of capital offences, over which the circuit courts alone have jurisdiction. The circuit courts are given appellate jurisdiction over the district courts; original jurisdiction in

civil cases such as are contemplated by the Constitution when the matter in dispute exceeds $500 in value; and unlimited criminal jurisdiction over cases falling within the purview of federal law.

255. **In criminal cases** there is, generally speaking, no appeal. In civil cases, appeal from the district to the circuit courts can be taken only when the matter in dispute exceeds $50 in value, from the circuit courts to the supreme court only when it exceeds $5000, except that cases of certain exceptional, specified classes may be appealed without respect to the amount involved. Any case which involves the interpretation of the Constitution can be taken to the supreme court, however small the sum in dispute.

256. **All Judges of the United States** are appointed by the President, with and by the consent and advice of the Senate, to serve during good behavior. There are in all fifty-six federal judicial districts, and for each of these a special district judge is appointed, though in large, thinly populated sections of the country it has sometimes been customary to have one judge hold court in several districts.

257. Federal judges of the inferior courts are, so to say, interchangeable. When necessary, a district judge can go into another district than his own and either aid or replace the district judge there; a district judge may also, when it seems necessary for the dispatch of business, sit as circuit judge; and a circuit judge may, in his turn, upon occasion hold district court. This seems the less anomalous when it is remembered that the earliest arrangement was, for the district judges to hold circuit court always in the absence of the justices of the supreme court from circuit, or in conjunction with them, and that special circuit judges were appointed only because of the necessity for more judges consequent upon a rapid increase of federal judicial business.

258. The salary of the chief justice of the United States is $10,500, that of each of the other justices, $10,000. Circuit court judges receive $6000, and district judges from $3500 to $5000.

259. **The District Attorney and the Marshal.** — Almost every district has its own federal *district attorney* and its own United States *marshal*, both of whom are appointed by the President. It is the duty of the federal district attorney to prosecute all offenders against the criminal laws of the United

States, to conduct all civil cases instituted in his district in behalf of the United States and to appear for the defence in all cases instituted against the United States, to appear in defence of revenue officers of the United States where they are sued for illegal action, etc. The marshal is the ministerial officer of the federal circuit and district courts. He executes all their orders and processes, arrests and keeps all prisoners charged with criminal violation of federal law, etc., and has within each state the same powers, within the scope of United States law, that the sheriff of that state has under the laws of the state. He is the federal sheriff.

260. The orders and processes of a state court are binding and operative only within the state to which the court belongs; the orders and processes of United States courts, on the contrary, are binding and operative over the entire Union.

261. **The courts of the District of Columbia and of the territories** are courts of the United States, but they are not federal courts; they bear, so far as their jurisdiction is concerned, the character of state and federal courts united. The only laws of the territories and of the District of Columbia are laws of the United States, inasmuch as the legislatures of the territories act under statutory grant from Congress.[1] The territorial legislatures are, so to say, commissioned by Congress; and the laws which they pass are administered by judges appointed by the President.

262. The territorial courts and the courts of the District of Columbia do not come within the view of the Constitution at all. With reference to them Congress acts under no limitations of power whatever. The rule of tenure during good behavior, for example, which applies to all judges of the United States appointed under the Constitution, does not apply to judges of the territories or of the District of Columbia. The term of office of territorial judges is fixed at four years. The federal courts sitting in the states, and the United States courts established in the territories, ought not to be thought of as parts of the same system, although the supreme court is the highest tribunal of appeal for both.

[1] Congress early enacted that the people of the District of Columbia should continue to live under the laws which had previously had force in the District when owned by Virginia and Maryland.

263. **The procedure of a federal court** follows, as a rule, the procedure of the courts of the state in which it is sitting; and state law is applied by the courts of the United States in all matters not touched by federal enactment. Juries are constituted, testimony taken, argument heard, etc., for the most part, according to the practice of the state courts; so that, so far as possible, both as regards the outward forms observed and the principles applied, a federal court is domestic, not foreign, to the state in which it acts.

264. It is not within the privilege of Congress to delegate to the courts of the states the functions of courts of the United States; for the Constitution distinctly provides that, besides the supreme court, there shall be no court authorized to exercise the judicial powers of the United States except such as Congress "may, from time to time, ordain and *establish.*" The adoption of state courts by Congress is, of course, excluded by plain implication. A very interesting contrast is thus established between the federal judicial system of the United States and the federal judicial systems of Germany and Switzerland (secs.* 436, 559).

265. **The Federal Executive.** — "The executive power," says the Constitution, "shall be vested in a President of the United States of America," who "shall hold his office during a term of four years." As a matter of fact, of course, it has proved practically impossible for a single man actually to exercise the whole executive power; the President is assisted by numerous heads of departments to whom falls so large a part of the actual duties of administration that it has become substantially correct to describe the President as simply presiding over and controlling by a general oversight the execution of the laws; which is doubtless all that the sagacious framers of the Constitution expected.

The Vice-President has no part in the executive function. He is the President's substitute, and is chosen at the same time and in the same manner that the President is chosen.

266. **Election of a President.** — The choice is not direct

by the people, but indirect, through electors chosen by the people. In each state there are elected as many electors as the state has representatives and senators in Congress, the "electoral vote" of each state being thus equal to its total representation in Congress.

> The electors are voted for on the Tuesday following the first Monday of November in the year which immediately precedes the expiration of a presidential term. They assemble in the several state capitals to cast their votes on the first Wednesday of the December following. Their votes are counted in the houses of Congress sitting in joint session on the second Wednesday of the following February. The President is inaugurated on the fourth of March next.

267. **Practical Operation of the Plan : the Party Conventions.** — The theory of this arrangement is that each elector really exercises an independent choice in the votes which he casts, voting for the men whom his own judgment has selected for the posts of President and Vice-President. In fact, however, the electors only register party decisions made during the previous summer in national conventions. Each party holds during that summer a great convention composed of party delegates from all parts of the Union, and nominates the candidates of its choice for the presidency and vice-presidency. The electors, again, are, in their turn, chosen according to the selections of party conventions in the several states; and the party which gains the most electors in the November elections puts its candidates into office through their votes, which are cast as a matter of course in obedience to the will of the party conventions. The party conventions are by far the most important part of the machinery of election.

268. **Qualifications for the Office of President.** — "No person, except a natural born citizen, or a citizen of the United States at the time of the adoption of this constitution shall be eligible to the office of president; neither shall any person be eligible to that office who shall not have attained to the age of thirty-five years, and been fourteen years a resident within the

United Stàtes."[1] In respect of age there is here only a slight advance upon the qualification required of a senator; in respect of citizenship it is of course very much more rigorous than in the case of members of Congress.

269. It is provided by the Constitution that the compensation received by judges of the United States shall not be diminished during their terms of office; concerning the President, whose tenure of office is much briefer, it is provided that his compensation shall neither be diminished *nor increased* during his term.

270. **Duties and Powers of the President.** — It is the duty of the President to see that the laws of the United States are faithfully executed; he is made commander-in-chief of the army and navy of the United States, and of the militia of the several states when called into the actual service of the United States; he is to regulate the foreign relations of the country, receiving all foreign ministers and being authorized to make treaties with the assent of two-thirds of the Senate; and he is to appoint and commission all officers of the federal government. The Constitution makes all his appointments subject to confirmation by the Senate; but it also gives Congress the power to remove from the superintending view of the Senate the filling of all inferior official positions by vesting the appointment of such subordinate officers as it thinks proper in the President alone, in the courts of law, or in the heads of departments. As a matter of fact, legislation has relieved the Senate of the supervision of the vast majority of executive appointments. The confirmation of the Senate is still necessary to the appointment of ambassadors, other public ministers, and consuls, of judges of the courts of the United States, of the chief departmental officials, of the principal post-office and customs officers, — of all the more important servants of the general government: but these of course constitute only a minority of all the persons receiving executive appointment: the majority are appointed without legislative oversight.

[1] Constitution, Art. II., sec. i., par. 5.

271. The unfortunate, the demoralizing influences which have been allowed to determine executive appointments since President Jackson's time have affected appointments made subject to the Senate's confirmation hardly less than those made without its co-operation: senatorial scrutiny has not proved effectual for securing the proper constitution of the public service. Indeed, the " courtesy of the Senate," — the so-called " courtesy " by which senators allowed appointments in the several states to be regulated by the preference of the senators of the predominant party from the states concerned, — at one time promised to add to the improper motives of the Executive the equally improper motives of the Senate.

272. **Reform of Methods of Appointment to Federal Offices.** — The attempts which have been made in recent years to reform by law the system of appointments have not been directed towards the higher offices filled with the consent of the Senate, but only towards those inferior offices which are filled by the single authority of the President or of the heads of the executive departments; have touched in their results, indeed, only the less important offices. The Act which became law in June, 1883, and which is known as the "Pendleton Act," may be said to cover only 'employees': it does not affect, that is, any person really *in authority*, though it does affect the large body of federal servants. It provides, in brief, for the appointment by the President, by and with the advice and consent of the Senate, of a *Civil Service Commission* consisting of three persons, not more than two of whom shall be adherents of the same political party, under whose recommendation as representatives of the President, selections shall be made for the lower grades of the federal service upon the basis of competitive examination. It forbids the solicitation of money from employees of the government for political uses and all active party service on the part of members of the civil administration: it endeavors, in short, to "take the civil service out of politics."

273. The carrying out of those portions of the Act which relate to the method of choosing public officers is, however, entirely subject to

the pleasure of the President. The Constitution vests in him the power of appointment, subject to no limitation except the possible advice and consent of the Senate. Any Act which assumes to prescribe the manner in which the President shall make his choice of public servants must, therefore, be merely advisory : the President may accept its directions or not as he pleases. The only force that can hold him to the observance of its principle is the force of public opinion.

274. **The Presidential Succession.** — In case of the removal, death, resignation, or disability of both the President and Vice-President, the office of President is to be filled *ad interim* by the Secretary of State, or, if he cannot act, by the Secretary of the Treasury, or, in case he cannot act, by the Secretary of War ; and so on, in succession, by the Attorney General, the Postmaster General, the Secretary of the Navy, or the Secretary of the Interior. None of these officers can act, however, unless he have the qualifications as to age, citizenship, and residence required by the Constitution of occupants of the presidential chair.

Until this arrangement was made, by act of Congress in 1886, the 'succession' passed first to the president *pro tempore* of the Senate, and, failing him, to the Speaker of the House of Representatives. This was found inconvenient because there are intervals now and again when there is neither a president *pro tempore* of the Senate nor a Speaker of the House.

275. **Relations of the Executive to Congress.** — The only provisions contained in the Constitution concerning the relation of the President to Congress are these: that "he shall, from time to time, give to the congress information of the state of the union, and recommend to their consideration such measures as he shall judge necessary and expedient" ; and that "he may, on extraordinary occasions, convene both houses, or either of them," in extra session, "and, in case of disagreement between them, with respect to the time of adjournment, he may adjourn them to such time as he shall think proper" (Art. II., sec. iii.). His power to inform Congress concerning the state of the union and to recommend to it the passage of measures is exercised only in the sending of annual and special written 'messages.'

276. Washington and John Adams interpreted the clause to mean that they might address Congress in person, as the sovereign in Eng-

land may do: their annual communications to Congress were spoken addresses. But Jefferson, the third President, being an ineffective speaker, this habit was discontinued and the fashion of written messages was inaugurated and firmly established. (Compare sec.* 679.) Possibly, had the President not so closed the matter against new adjustments, this clause of the Constitution might legitimately have been made the foundation for a much more habitual and informal, and yet at the same time much more public and responsible, interchange of opinion between the Executive and Congress. Having been interpreted, however, to exclude the President from any but the most formal and ineffectual utterance of perfunctory advice, our federal executive and legislature have been shut off from co-operation and mutual confidence to an extent to which no other modern system furnishes a parallel. In all other modern governments the heads of the administrative departments are given the right to sit in the legislative body and to take part in its proceedings. The legislature and executive are thus associated in such a way that the ministers of state can lead the houses without dictating to them, and the ministers themselves be controlled without being misunderstood, — in such a way that the two parts of the government which should be most closely co-ordinated, the part, namely, by which the laws are made and the part by which the laws are executed, may be kept in close harmony and intimate co-operation, with the result of giving coherence to the action of the one and energy to the action of the other.

277. The Executive Departments. — The Constitution does not provide for the creation of executive departments, but it takes it for granted that such departments will be founded. Thus it says (Art. II., sec. ii., par. 1, 2) that the President "may require the opinion, in writing, of the principal officer in each of the executive departments, upon any subject relating to the duties of their respective offices," and that Congress may vest the appointment of such inferior officers as it may see fit "in the heads of departments." The executive departments consequently owe their creation and organization to statute only.

278. The first Congress erected four such departments, namely, the departments of State, of the Treasury, of War, and of Justice. In 1798 the management of the navy, which had at first been included in the duties of the War Department,

was entrusted to a special Department of the Navy; in 1829 the post office, which had been a subdivision of the Treasury, was created an independent Department; and in 1849 a Department of the Interior was organized to receive a miscellany of functions not easy to classify, except in the feature of not belonging properly within any department previously created.

> A similar character, it is interesting to remark, may be attributed to some corresponding department, bearing either this name or a name of like significance, in almost every other modern government. There is everywhere a department of state to receive functions not otherwise specially disposed of.

279. In 1889 there was added to these a Department of Agriculture. We have, thus, at present, eight executive departments, viz.: (1) **A Department of State,** which is what would be called in most other governments our "foreign office," having charge of all the relations of the United States with foreign countries.

280. (2) **A Department of the Treasury,** which is the financial agency of the government, and whose functions cover the collection of the public revenues accruing through the customs duties and the taxes on whiskey and tobacco, their safe keeping and their disbursement in accordance with the appropriations from time to time made by Congress; the auditing of the accounts of all departments; the supervision and regulation of the national banks and of the currency of the United States; the coinage of money; and the collection of certain industrial and other statistics.

> This Department, therefore, contains within it the treasury and comptrolling functions which in the states are separated.
> 281. To this Department is attached also the *Bureau of Printing and Engraving,* by which all the printing of public documents, etc., is done.

282. (3) **A Department of War,** which has charge of the military forces of the Union;

283. (4) **A Department of the Navy,** which has charge of the naval forces of the general government;

284. (5) **A Department of Justice,** from which emanates all the legal advice of which the federal authorities stand in need at any time, and to which is entrusted the supervision of the conduct of all litigation in which the United States may be concerned. To it are subordinate all the marshals and district attorneys of the United States, — all ministerial, non-judicial law officers, that is, in the service of the government. It may be compendiously described as the lawyer force of the government. It is presided over by an Attorney General, all the other departments, except the Post Office, being under 'Secretaries.'

285. (6) **A Post Office Department,** under a Postmaster General, which is charged with the carrying and delivery of letters and parcels, with the transmission of money by means of certain 'money orders' and notes issued by the Department, or under cover of a careful system of registration, and with making the proper postal arrangements with foreign countries.

> These arrangements with foreign countries may be made without the full formalities of treaty, the consent of the President alone being necessary for the ratification of international agreements made by the Postmaster General for the facilitation of the functions of the Department. The United States is a member of the Universal Postal Union, to which most of the civilized countries of the world belong. The central office of this Union is under the management of the Swiss administration. Its administrative expenses are defrayed by contribution of the various governments belonging to the Union.

286. (7) **A Department of the Interior,** which has charge (i.) Of the taking of the Census, as from time to time ordered by Congress in accordance with the provision of the Constitution (Art. I., sec. i., par. 3) which makes it the duty of Congress to have a census taken every ten years as a basis for the redistribution of representation in the House of Representatives among the several states; (ii.) Of the management of

the public lands (*General Land Office*); (iii.) Of the government's dealings with the Indians, a function which is exercised through a special Commissioner of Indian Affairs in Washington and various agencies established in different parts of the Indian country.

> It is through this *Indian Bureau*, for example, that all laws concerning the settlement, assistance, or supervision of the tribes are administered, as well as all laws concerning the payment of claims made upon the federal government for compensation for depredations committed by the Indians, and laws touching the distribution and tenure of land among the Indians.

(iv.) Of the paying of pensions and the distribution of bounty lands, a function which it exercises through a special *Commissioner of Pensions;* (v.) Of the issuing and recording of patents and the preservation of the models of all machines patented: for the performance of these duties there is a *Patent Office;* (vi.) Of the keeping and distribution of all public documents (*Superintendent of Public Documents*); (vii.) Of the auditing of the accounts of certain railway companies, to which the United States government has granted loans or subsidies, and the enforcing of the laws passed by Congress with reference to such roads (*Office of the Commissioner of Railroads*); (viii.) Of the collection of statistical and other information concerning education, and the diffusion of the information so collected for the purpose of aiding the advance and systematization of education throughout the country (*The Office of Education*); (ix.) Of the superintendence of the government hospital for the insane and the Columbia Asylum for the Deaf and Dumb.

> Many of these subdivisions of the Interior, though in strictness subject to the oversight and control of the Secretary of the Interior, have in reality a very considerable play of independent movement.

287. (8) **A Department of Agriculture,** which is charged with furthering in every possible way, by the collection of information not only, but also by the prosecution of scientific

investigation with reference to the diseases of plants, etc., the agricultural interests of the country, and under which there is maintained a special *Forestry Division.*

288.   Set apart to themselves, and therefore without represcutation in the Cabinet, there are (1) The *Department of Labor,* which is charged with the collection and publication of statistical and other information touching the condition and interests of laborers, — information, for instance, bearing upon the relations of labor and capital, hours of labor, the housing of laborers, rates of wages and methods of payment, the food and expenses of laborers, etc.   (2) The *Interstate Commerce Commission,* a semi-judicial body by which the federal statutes forbidding unjust discriminations in railway rates in interstate freight or passenger traffic, prohibiting certain sorts of combinations in railroad management, etc., are interpreted and enforced.   (3) The *Civil Service Commission* by which the Act mentioned in sec. 1104 is administered.   (4) The *Commission of Fish and Fisheries,* whose duty it is to make the necessary investigations and prosecute the necessary measures for the preservation, improvement, and increase of the stock of fish in our rivers and lakes and on our coasts.

Some Representative Authorities.

On the institutional development of the colonial period:

Hildreth, R., "History of the United States from the discovery of America to the End of the Sixteenth Congress" (1821).   First Series. 3 vols. 8vo. New ed. N. Y., 1879.

Bancroft, George, "History of the United States," from the discovery of America to the adoption of the federal Constitution.   6 vols. 8vo. N. Y.

Doyle, J. A., "English Colonies in America," to the end of the seventeenth century. 3 vols. 8vo. N. Y., 1882, 1888.

Lodge, H. C., "A Short History of the English Colonies in America."
N. Y., 1881.

Frothingham, "The Rise of the Republic of the United States." Boston, 1872.

Curtis, G. T., "History of the Origin, Formation, and Adoption of the Constitution of the United States." 2 vols. N. Y., 1854, 1858. In this connection only the first volume is pertinent.

Scott, E. G., "Development of Constitutional Liberty in the English Colonies of America." N.Y., 1882.

On the formation of the Union:

Curtis, G. T., as above. Vol. II.

Bancroft, George, as above. Vol. VI.

Fiske, John, "The Critical Period of American History." Boston, 1888.

Johnston, Alexander, "The First Century of the Constitution," in the *New Princeton Review,* September, 1887.

McMaster, J. B., "History of the People of the United States." Vol. I. N. Y., 1883.

Pitkin, Timothy, "Political and Civil History of the United States of America from their Commencement to the Close of the Administration of Washington." 2 vols. 8vo. New Haven, 1828.

Adams, H. B., "Maryland's Influence upon Land Cessions to the United States," in Johns Hopkins University Studies in Historical and Political Science. Third Series, No. I.

American Statesmen Series: volumes on John Adams and Thomas Jefferson, by *J. T. Morse, Jr.;* on Alexander Hamilton and on George Washington by *H. C. Lodge;* on Patrick Henry by *M. C. Tyler;* and on James Madison by *S. H. Gay.*

On institutional development under the Constitution:

Hildreth, R., as above. Second Series. 3 vols.

Schouler, James, "History of the United States of America under the Constitution." 4 vols. Washington, 1880–1887.

v. Holst, H., "The Constitutional and Political History of the United States." Translated from the German by A. B. Mason, J. J. Lalor, and Paul Shorey. 5 vols. 8vo. Chicago, 1876–1887.

Johnston, Alexander, "History of American Politics." N. Y., revised ed., 1882.

Adams, Henry (editor), "Documents relating to New England Federalism." Boston, 1877.

Benton, T. H., "Thirty Years' View; or, A History of the Working of the American Government for Thirty Years, 1820–1850." 2 vols. 8vo. N. Y., 1854–1856.

American Statesmen Series: volumes on J. Q. Adams by *J. T. Morse, Jr.;* on T. H. Benton and on Gouverneur Morris by *Theodore Roosevelt;* on J. C. Calhoun by *H. v. Holst;* on H. Clay by *Carl Schurz;* on A. Gallatin by *J. A. Stevens;* on A. Jackson by *W. G. Sumner;* on John Marshall by *A. B. Magruder;* on J. Monroe by *D. C. Gilman;* on J. Randolph by *H. Adams;* on M. Van Buren by *E. M. Shepard;* and on D. Webster by *H. C. Lodge.*

Roosevelt, Theodore, "The Winning of the West." 2 vols. N. Y., 1889.

Winsor, Justin (editor), "Narrative and Critical History of America." Vol. VII. Boston, 1888. Contains full bibliographical notes.

Sumner, W. G., "Politics in America, 1776–1876." A centennial summary. *North American Review,* January, 1876, p. 47.

On the character of the federal government under the Constitution:

The controversial literature preceding and accompanying the War of Secession may be found, representatively, in

Jefferson, Thomas, "Works."

Adams, John, "Works."

Calhoun, J. C., "Works."

Webster, Daniel, "Speeches."

Stephens, Alexander, "A Constitutional View of the War between the States." 2 vols. 8vo. Philadelphia, 1868.

Centz, P. C. (B. J. Sage), "The Republic of Republics." Boston, 4 ed., 1881.

Hurd, J. C., "The Theory of Our National Existence." Boston, 1881.

Brownson, O. A., "The American Republic; its Constitution, Tendencies, and Destiny." N. Y., 1866 and 1886.

Disassociated with the issues of the Civil War are the following:

The Federalist, by Alexander Hamilton, James Madison, and John Jay.

Story, Joseph, "Commentaries on the Constitution." Edited by
T. M. Cooley.

Cooley, T. M., "Treatise on the Constitutional Limitations which rest
upon the Legislative Power of the States of the American Union."
Boston, 2 ed., 1871.
"The General Principles of Constitutional Law in the United
States of America." Boston, 1880.

v. Holst, H., "Das Staatsrecht dèr Vereinigten Staaten von America"
in *Marquardsen's* "Handbuch des Oeffentlichen Rechts." Frei-
burg in B., 1885. Translated under the title, "The Constitutional Law of the United States of America." By A. B. Mason.
Chicago, 1887.

de Tocqueville, A., "Democracy in America." Translated by Henry
Reeve. London, new ed., 1875.

Dicey, A. V., "Lectures Introductory to the Study of the Law of the
Constitution." London, 1886. This book, though a commentary
on the English Constitution, contains much excellent comment
also on our own.

Bryce, James, "The American Commonwealth." 2 vols. London,
1888.

Maine, Sir H. S., "Popular Government." N. Y., 1886, especially
Chap. IV.

Wilson, Woodrow, "Congressional Government, A Study in American Politics." Boston, 1885.

On the governments of the States and Local Government:

Jameson, J. F., "Introduction to the Constitutional and Political
History of the Individual States." In the Johns Hopkins Uni-
versity Studies in Historical and Political Science. Fourth
Series, No. V.

Poore, Ben: P., "Federal and State Constitutions, Colonial Charters,
and other Organic Laws of the United States." 2 vols. Washington, 1877.

Stimson, F. J., "American Statute Law." A Digest. Boston, 1886.

Johns Hopkins University Studies in Historical and Political Science:
First Series: "An Introduction to American Institutional History," by *E. A. Freeman;* "The Germanic Origin of New England Towns," by *H. B. Adams;* "Local Government in Illinois,"

by *A. Shaw;* "Saxon Tithingmen in America," and "Norman Constables in America," by *H. B. Adams;* "Local Government in Michigan and the Northwest," by *E. W. Bemis;* "Parish Institutions of Maryland," by *E. Ingle;* "Old Maryland Manors," by *John Johnson;* "Village Communities of Cape Anne and Salem," by *H. B. Adams;* "The Genesis of a New England State," by *Alexander Johnston;* "Local Government and Free Schools in South Carolina," by *B. J. Ramage. Second Series:* "Samuel Adams, the Man of the Town Meeting," by *J. K. Hosmer;* "Institutional Beginnings in a Western State," by *Jesse Macy;* "Town and County Government in the English Colonies of North America," by *E. Channing. Third Series:* "Virginia Local Institutions," by *E. Ingle;* "Local Institutions of Maryland," by *L. W. Wilhelm;* "Influence of the Proprietors in founding the State of New Jersey," by *Austin Scott;* "American Constitutions," by *Horace Davis. Fourth Series:* "Town Government in Rhode Island," by *W. E. Foster;* "The Narragansett Planters," by *E. Channing;* "Pennsylvania Boroughs," by *W. P. Holcomb;* "The Puritan Colony at Annapolis, Maryland," by *D. R. Randall;* "The Land System of the New England Colonies," by *M. Egleston.*

Parker, Joel, 'Jaffrey Address.' 1873. ' Origin, Organization, and Influence of the Towns of New England," in Proceedings Mass. Hist. Soc., June, 1886.

Carter, C. H., "Connecticut Boroughs." New Haven Hist. Soc., Vol. IV.

Spencer, D., "Local Government in Wisconsin." Wis. Hist. Soc'y's Collections, Vol. II.

"Shires and Shire Towns in the South." *Lippincott's Magazine.* August, 1882.

Ford, W. C., "The American Citizen's Manual." Part I. N. Y., 1882.

Hosmer, J. K., "Samuel Adams," in American Statesmen Series. Boston, 1885.

INDEX.

SUPPLEMENTARY TO THE TOPICAL ANALYSIS.

[The references are to sections.]

Agriculture, Department of, 287.

Amendment of state constitutions, 67–72 ; of the federal constitution, 214.

America, the English occupation of, 1.

Arsenals and dockyards of the U. S., 220.

Articles of Confederation, The, 35.

Assemblies, the colonial, in Va., 14 ; their development, 23, 24.

Auditor, The, of a state, 158, 160.

Bankruptcy, Laws of, in the U. S., 77.

Boroughs, 198 *et seq.*

Burke, Edmund, on the development of the colonial assemblies in America, 23.

Cabinet, the federal, 141, 277 *et seq.*

Charters, colonial, 17–19.

Cities, 198 *et seq.* ; their organization, 203–205.

Citizenship in the U. S., 84, 85 ; elements of confusion touching, 86 ; naturalization, 87 ; under a confederation, 89.

Civil Service Reform, 271–273 ; Commission, 288.

Colonial organization, English, in New England, 9 ; expansion without separation in the South, 11 ; society in the South, 12.

Colonies, the English, in New England, 4–9 ; in the South, 10–15 ; the Middle Atlantic, 16 ; development of constitutional liberty in the, 23–25 ; their political sympathy, 26 ; separateness of their governments, 33.

Columbia, District of, 217, 219 ; the courts of the, 261, 262.

Commerce, inter-state, the regulation of, 81 ; Commission, 288.

Commission, the inter-state Commerce, 288.

Committees, Standing, in state legislatures, 105 ; in federal Senate, 230–232 ; in the federal House of Representatives, 240–244.

Common Law courts in the states, 113–122.

Governors, of the states, 133; their terms of office, 136; their qualifications, 137; their relations to other state officials, 141–145, 162; their duties and powers, 147–150.

House of Representatives, see Representatives, House of.
Houses, reasons for two legislative, in U. S., 97–100; names of the two legislative, in the states, 102.

Interior, Department of the, 286.
Inter-state commerce, regulation of, in U. S,. 81; the, Commission, 288.

Judges, election of, in the states, 128, 129; qualifications required of them, 130; appointment and tenure of federal, 256; their relations to each other, 257; their salaries, 258.
Jurisdiction (judicial) of the U. S., 250; of existing federal courts, 253–255.
Justice, administration of, in the states, 109–131; under the federal government, 250–264.
Justice, Department of, 284.

Labor, Department of, 288.
Law of the states, its character, 55, 56; its scope, 58 *et seq.*; its conflicts, 73–79.
Legislation, distrust of, in the states, 64; course of, in the state legislatures, 104, 105; course of, in Congress, 230–232, 240–249.
Legislatures of the states, 92–95; not sovereign bodies, 96; their development, 23, 24.
Liberty, development of constitutional, in the colonies, 23–25.
Local government in the states, 142–146, 162 *et seq.*
Louisiana, peculiar character of the laws of, 80.

Marshal, the federal, 259, 260.
Massachusetts, charter of colonial, 17.
Ministers, the federal, their relations to Congress, 232, 244.
Municipal Councils, 204, 205.

National Idea, growth of the, 45 *et seq.*
Naturalization, 87.
Navy, Department of the, 283.
New Mexico, the laws of, 80.

Opinion, effects of, upon character of the federal government, 42 *et seq.*

Outline Maps of the United States.

Prepared by EDWARD CHANNING, Ph.D., and ALBERT B. HART, Ph.D., Instructors in History in Harvard College.

Description.

The **Large Map** is printed on strong white paper, in four sections, each 26 × 42 inches; the sections are divided by the 95th meridian and the 37th parallel. They may be used separately or pasted together. There is no lettering upon the map, except the numbering of the parallels and meridians, — the location of the principal cities being indicated by dots. Price, 15 cts. per section; 50 cts. complete.

The **Small Map** is printed on tough white paper, in blue ink, and is 11½ × 18 inches in size, including a broad margin on the right-hand side, which furnishes space for written comments. The names of the principal rivers and the numbers of the parallels and meridians appear on this map. Price, 2 cts. each; $1.50 per hundred.

Application.

Physical Geography. By the simple use of shading and colors, the maps may be made the basis of reproductions or original sketches of physical geography, thus saving the cost of elaborate wall and other maps, and allowing teachers to exercise their individual knowledge.

Geology. They are also in use to illustrate geological lessons and lectures.

Meteorology. Conditions of climate, isotherms, and isobares may be shown upon the maps with great ease.

Statistical Maps. The increasing use of maps for exhibiting economic facts is facilitated by the use of these outlines. The maps in the Census Reports and Scribner's Statistical Atlas may be reproduced. on the same or a larger scale. Among the subjects capable of this form of illustration are: the distribution of population; race elements; language elements; illiteracy; the distribution of manufactures, wealth, agricultural products; etc., etc.

Political Maps. As a basis for historical and political maps. the boundaries of the present States and Territories appear on the maps in faint lines. The pupil is thus taught to connect obsolete divisions with those now existing. A great variety of special maps may be drawn, among them the following: the Colonies and the United States at successive epochs; the distribution of electoral votes; the distribution of votes in Congress on the tariff and other important questions; annexation of territory; divisions into sections; divisions created by the great compromises; the Confederate States; etc., etc.

[OVER.

HISTORY.

Sheldon's General History. For high school and college. The only history following the "seminary" or laboratory plan now advocated by all leading teachers. Price, $1.60.

Sheldon's Greek and Roman History. Contains the first 250 pages of the above book. Price, $1.00.

Teacher's Manual to Sheldon's History. Puts into the instructor's hand the *key* to the above system. Price, 80 cents

Sheldon's Aids to the Teaching of General History. Gives list of essential books for reference library. Price, 10 cents.

Bridgman's Ten Years of Massachusetts. Pictures the development of the Commonwealth as seen in its laws. Price, 75 cents.

Shumway's A Day in Ancient Rome. With 59 illustrations. Should find a place as a *supplementary reader* in every high school class studying Cicero, Horace, Tacitus, etc. Price, 75 cents.

Old South Leaflets on U. S. History. Reproductions of important political and historical papers, accompanied by useful notes. Price, 5 cents each. Per hundred, $3.00.

    This general series of Old South Leaflets now includes the following subjects: The Constitution of the United States, The Articles of Confederation, The Declaration of Independence, Washington's Farewell Address, Magna Charta, Vane's "Healing Question," Charter of Massachusetts Bay, 1629, Fundamental Orders of Connecticut, 1638, Franklin's Plan of Union, 1754, Washington's Inaugurals, Lincoln's Inaugurals and Emancipation Proclamation, The Federalist, Nos. 1 and 2, The Ordinance of 1787, The Constitution of Ohio, Washington's Letter to Benjamin Harrison, Washington's Circular Letter to the Governors.

Allen's History Topics. Covers Ancient, Modern, and American history, and gives an excellent list of books of reference. Price, 25 cents.

Fisher's Select Bibliog. of Ecclesiastical History. An annotated list of the most essential books for a Theological studen't library. Price, 15 cents.

Hall's Methods of Teaching History. "Its excellence and helpfulness ought to secure it many readers." — *The Nation.* Price, $1.30.

Wilson's the State. Elements of Historical and Practical Politics. A text-book for advanced classes in high schools and colleges on the organization and functions of governments. *In Press.*

D. C. HEATH & CO., Publishers,

BOSTON, NEW YORK AND CHICAGO.

Lightning Source UK Ltd.
Milton Keynes UK
UKHW010256231118
332756UK00012B/1910/P